VICIOUS CIRCLES AND INFINITY

VICIOUS CIRCLES
AND
INFINITY

A Panoply of Paradoxes

PATRICK HUGHES
and
GEORGE BRECHT

1975
Doubleday & Company, Inc.
Garden City, New York

Library of Congress Cataloging in Publication Data

Hughes, Patrick, 1939–
  Vicious circles and infinity.

  Bibliography: p. 95
  1. Paradox. 2. Paradoxes. I. Brecht, George,
joint author. II. Title.
BC199.P2H83   165
ISBN 0-385-09917-7
Library of Congress Catalog Card Number 74–17611

810234

To Molly and I

ACKNOWLEDGMENTS

The authors would like to acknowledge the help they have had from Roger Woolhouse, Anthony Hill, Ian Breakwell, Paul Hammond, Trevor Winkfield, Cornelius Cardew, Martin Gardner, Eric Thacker, Jasia Reichardt, John Sharkey, Steve Adamson, Jenny Towndrow, George Melhuish, Philip Hughes, Les Coleman, David Sylvester, Suzi Gablik, John Timbers, Tony Earnshaw, John Lyle, Angela Flowers, Bill Gainham, David Huffman, Roland Penrose, Hilary Rubinstein, Doug Sandle, Robert Short, Mme. Georgette Magritte, E. H. Gombrich, Arturo Schwarz, Roy Bignell, William Copley, Marcel Mariën, Alan Fletcher, Christine Hammond. The authors are also thankful to their editor, John Ware, for his zestful aid and understanding.

The authors would like to thank Basil Blackwell & Mott Ltd. for permission to reprint from *Analysis* and *Mind;* The Clarendon Press, Oxford, for permission to quote from J. A. Benardete's *Infinity;* Simon and Schuster, Inc. for permission to quote from Bertrand Russell's *My Philosophical Development;* Little, Brown and Company in association with The Atlantic Monthly Press for permission to quote from Bertrand Russell's *Autobiography,* Vol. 1; Grove Press for permission to quote from Tom Stoppard's *Jumpers.* They are particularly grateful to Martin Gardner for permission to quote him on Hempel, and the surprise inspection.

ADVERTISEMENT

This is the first anthology of paradoxes.

It is the first time the paradoxes of self-reference and of infinity have been collected together.

This is the first time examples of paradoxical visual art and illusion, and paradoxical aphorisms, have been united with the logical paradoxes and paradoxical philosophy.

It is a very complete collection of paradoxes, and it includes a full bibliography for further study.

The anthology includes a study in depth of the logicians at work on the paradox of the Surprise Inspection.

Some of the paradoxes in this book may seem difficult, trivial, or repetitive—they sometimes seemed so to the authors—but they have nevertheless been included for the sake of completeness.

The anthology has no particular ax to grind, apart from that of having no particular ax to grind.

This is not necessarily a book to be read sequentially—it can be used to dip into.

INTRODUCTION

We hope you enjoy the paradoxes, verbal and visual, as much as we do. We have tried to let the paradoxes speak for themselves. The ratio of comment to material is great in the field of paradox: the paradoxes are few and brief, the commentaries many and lengthy. As is often the case, it is easier to talk about a thing than it is to do it.

One of the bonds between the authors of this book is the sense of humor; perhaps the paradoxes should be seen in this light.

Patrick Hughes

George Brecht

VICIOUS CIRCLES AND INFINITY

The literature about paradoxes is marred by persistent attempts to explain the paradoxes away. Our intention here is a more modest, descriptive one. Using several examples of propositions approaching the paradoxical state, we will attempt to show what conditions go for the making of a logical paradox. Often consideration of a poor example, by virtue of its imperfection, tells one more than consideration of a prime example, in its perfection. For us, all the paradoxes in this book add up to a definition of what a paradox is.

The three terms of description (or condition) of a logical paradox most often used are *self-reference, contradiction,* and *vicious circle.*

There are many propositions which are *self-referential.* For instance: **This sentence has five words.**
> **This is a sentence.**
> **This sentence is written in the English language.**

1

Clearly none of these propositions are paradoxical, they are merely banal.

With regard to the second of our three terms, *contradiction,* we must pass over those propositions which are merely contradictory, e.g., **The planet Earth is not inhabited by men,** and look at those specific cases where there is self-reference and contradiction, which we might call self-contradiction. In its mildest form self-contradiction leads to propositions like these:

> **This sentence has six words.**
> **This is not a sentence.**
> **This sentence is written in the French language.**

These propositions refer to themselves and contradict themselves, but they are not paradoxes. However, there are forms of self-reference and contradiction of a stronger variety which approach the paradoxical state. A good example of this kind of contradiction is:

To do as it says, you must not have done as it says. There are several examples of these "not quite paradoxes" which appear to lack our third term of description, *vicious circularity.* These contradictions which follow, of the "Please Ignore This Notice" variety, do go round in a circle, but they don't go round and round. One might say that they are paradoxical, but that they are not paradoxes.

The following are not quite paradoxes, are circular contradictions, but lacking vicious circularity.

All rules have exceptions.

The general proposition of Oliver Wendell Holmes, Jr., that **"No general proposition is worth a damn!"**

Never say never.

How can a witness reply to a lawyer who says: **"Please answer yes or no to the following question—will the next word you speak be no?"**

An exchange from N. F. Simpson's play *The Form.*
Mr. Chacterson: **I wonder—if I might just put a supplementary question, Dr. Whinby—I wonder whether you would mind telling me—simply for the record—if there is any question you think might possibly come up in the foreseeable future to which you would reply unhesitatingly in the negative?**
James Whinby: (without hesitation) **Quite definitely not!**[1]

A crocodile snatched a baby from its mother and offered to return it if the mother could correctly answer the question: "Will I eat your baby?" If the mother had said "No" there would have been no difficulty but she was clever

enough to say "Yes" (if the crocodile were now to eat the baby, proving the mother right, he would be contradicting his offer to return the baby if the mother answered correctly).

It is forbidden to forbid (wall in Paris, May 1968).

A young lawyer had the following agreement with his teacher, Protagoras: if he won his first case he would pay for his instruction; if he lost, he would not pay. The youth kept refusing to accept cases until Protagoras forced the issue by suing him. Naturally the young man defended himself. If the young man lost he would not pay and if he won he would not pay.

Poaching on the hunting preserves of a powerful prince was punishable by death, but the prince further decreed that anyone caught poaching was to be given the privilege of deciding whether he would be hanged or beheaded. The culprit was permitted to make a statement—if it were false, he was to be hanged; if it were true, he was to be beheaded. One logical rogue availed himself of this dubious prerogative—to be hanged if he didn't and beheaded if he did— by stating "I shall be hanged." Here was a dilemma not anticipated. For, as the poacher put it, "If you now hang me you break the laws made by the prince, for my statement is true and I ought to be beheaded; but if you behead me you are also breaking the laws for then what I said was false and I should therefore be hanged."

In Chapter 51 of the second book of *Don Quixote*, Sancho Panza is confronted by a similar paradox. The owner of a large manor, on the island of Barataria, requires every man who enters his estate to announce the purpose of his visit. If the man tells the truth, he is unmolested; if he lies, he is hanged. A whimsical joker has answered the question by saying he intends to be hanged on the gallows he sees ahead of him. As governor of the island, Sancho has sworn to uphold the local laws. In this case, if he permits the hanging, the man will be hanged unjustly because he told the truth, but if he lets the man go free, the man deserves to hang.

Groucho Marx once said that he refused to join any club that would have him for a member.

There was only one catch and that was Catch-22, which specified that a concern for one's own safety in the face of dangers that were real and immediate was the process of a rational mind. Orr was crazy and could be grounded. All he had to do was ask; and as soon as he did, he would no longer be crazy and would have to fly more missions. Orr would be crazy to fly more missions and sane if he didn't, but if he was sane he had to fly them. If he flew them he was crazy and didn't have to; but if he didn't want to he was sane and had to.[2]

The following resolutions were passed by the Board of Councilmen in Canton, Mississippi:

5

1. Resolved, by this Council, that we build a new Jail.
2. Resolved, that the new Jail be built out of the materials of the old Jail.
3. Resolved, that the old Jail be used until the new Jail is finished.

Thomas Storer has used self-contradiction to manufacture an infallible machine:

Miniac: world's smallest electronic brain

In this age of computers, it seems a pity that sincere but impecunious scholars should be deprived of their benefits. Herewith are presented do-it-yourself plans for constructing a computer that will answer questions not resolvable by any other present machine. Among its many advantages, MINIAC is (1) small enough to be carried in one's watch pocket; (2) inexpensive; (3) infallible; (4) easy to build; (5) child's play to operate.

To build MINIAC:

1. Obtain a penny. (The substitution of a ha'penny will not materially affect MINIAC's operation.)

2. Typewrite the words YES and NO on two pieces of paper and glue one to each side of the penny.

To operate MINIAC:

1. Hold MINIAC on the thumb and forefinger (either hand, either side up) and ask it question A (e.g., "Will it rain tomorrow?").

2. Flip MINIAC and allow it to come to rest.

3. Note the answer, either YES or NO.

Now MINIAC has given us either a true answer or a false answer. To determine which:

6

4. Hold MINIAC as in operating instruction 1, ask the question B: "Will your present answer have the same truth-value as your previous answer?" and flip.

5. Note MINIAC's response to this question, either YES or NO.

Suppose MINIAC's answer to question B is YES. This is either a true answer or a false answer. If true, then it is true that the answer to question A has the same truth-value as the answer to question B, hence the answer to question A was a true answer; if false, then it is false that the answer to question A has the same truth-value as the answer to question B (which is false), hence the answer to question A was a true answer. In either case, if MINIAC answers YES to question B, then its answer to question A was a true answer. If MINIAC answers question B with NO, a similar line of reasoning shows that its answer to question A was a false answer.

The electronic character of MINIAC is obvious from the fact that there are two free electrons in the outer shell of the copper atom.[3]

Compare these "not quite paradoxes" with Bertrand Russell's full paradox of 1918, that of the barber:

"A man of Seville is shaved by the Barber of Seville if and only if the man does not shave himself. Does the Barber of Seville shave himself?"
If he does, he doesn't; AND if he doesn't, he does. Consider the notice: **"Please Ignore This Notice"**: to do as it says, you must not have done as it says. This is the differ-

ence between circularity in the "not quite paradoxes" and *vicious circularity* in the complete paradoxes.

The first, and in many ways the best, example of the full paradox is the paradox of the liar.

Eubulides, the Megarian sixth century B.C. Greek philosopher, and successor to Euclid, invented the paradox of the liar. In this paradox **Epimenides, the Cretan, says, "All Cretans are liars."** If he is telling the truth he is lying; and if he is lying, he is telling the truth. In the simpler form, **"I am lying,"** this paradox was known to the ancients as the pseudomenon.

There are several variations of this paradox:

This sentence is false.

W. V. O. Quine suggests: **"Yields a falsehood when appended to its own quotation" yields a falsehood when appended to its own quotation.**

This is a medieval formulation:
Socrates: "What Plato is about to say is false."
Plato: "Socrates has just spoken truly."

Alfred Tarski reports:
A book of one hundred pages, with just one sentence printed on each page.
On page 1 we read: **"The sentence printed on page 2 of this book is true."**

8

On page 2 we read: **"The sentence printed on page 3 of this book is true."**

And so it goes on up to page 99. However, on page 100, the last page of the book, we find: **"The sentence printed on page 1 of this book is false."**

It is false that there
is a true statement
within the rectangle
of Fig. 1.

Fig. 1

A. P. Ushenko says:

"According to Russell's treatment the sentence within the rectangle of Fig. 1 is meaningless, and may be called a pseudo-statement, because it is a version of the liar-paradox. But Russell's treatment is unsatisfactory because it resolves the original paradox at the price of a new one. For, if the sentence of Fig. 1 is meaningless we must admit, since we observe that there are no other sentences within the rectangle, that it is false that there is a genuine or meaningful statement within the rectangle of Fig. 1. And, if there is no statement within the rectangle of Fig. 1 then *it is false that there is a true statement within the rectangle of Fig. 1.* The italicized part of the preceding sentence will be recognized as identical with (even if a different token of) the sentence within the rectangle of Fig. 1. And since the italicized sentence is true, and therefore a meaningful statement, the sentence within the rectangle is not a pseudo-statement either. Thus, if the sentence in question is meaningless, then it is meaningful and vice versa."[4]

The English mathematician P. E. B. Jourdain in 1913 suggested the following:
On one side of a blank card print: **The statement on the other side of this card is true.**
On the opposite side of the same card print: **The statement on the other side of this card is false.**

Unfortunately, at the same time he proposed a card with, on one side: **The statement on the other side of this card is false.**
And on the other side: **The statement on the other side of this card is false.**[5]

Now most people agree that this is not fully paradoxical. It does not represent a *vicious* circle. This second card of Jourdain's does not attack *itself*. The two sentences *merely* contradict each other.

Oddly enough Russell chose to use this inferior version in his *Autobiography,* though he later recognized he had made a mistake. This mistake may be connected with Russell's feelings of disgust with the paradoxes, to which we shall refer later on.

However, Maurice Harvey has claimed that in the case of Jourdain's "second" card, with "false" on both sides, it is not merely that we don't know which sentence is true, nor even that it is inherently impossible to decide, but that

10

either decision, though coherent in itself, is inseparable from its own contradiction. He says, "We have a situation in which each sentence, besides asserting its own truth by convention, asserts only the falsity of another which denies it, and so reasserts its own truth."[6]

In his discussion of the medieval paradox already mentioned,

Socrates: "What Plato is about to say is false."
Plato: "Socrates has just spoken truly."

and of Jourdain's paradoxical card, in the classic formulation, when one side says: **The statement on the other side of this card is true,** and the other side says: **The statement on the other side of this card is false,** Martin Gardner, in an article in the *Antioch Review,* "Logical Paradoxes," says: "There is no self-reference in either form of the paradox."[7] We believe Gardner is mistaken. It would be true to say that what Socrates says or what Plato says or what is said on either side of Jourdain's card is not *self-referential,* but it would also be true to say that what Socrates says or what Plato says or what is said on either side of Jourdain's card is not *paradoxical.* But the *entity* of Socrates' remark and Plato's remark and the *entity* of both sides of Jourdain's card are *paradoxical,* and the paradox of Socrates' and Plato's remarks and the paradox of both sides of Jourdain's card are *self-referential.*

Valdis Augstkalns has proposed an absolute refutation of Jourdain's paradox. He suggests "a strip of paper with **The statement on the other side of this paper is true** written

11

on one side of it, and **The statement on the other side of this paper is false** written on the other side of it. The paradox in this form is quite vulnerable to an absolute refutation. One takes the paper, gives it a half twist, and joins the ends to form a Möbius strip. The serious and philosophically legitimate question is transformed to 'Eminent members of the panel, which is the other side of the paper?' "[8]

With the revival of logic in the second half of the nineteenth century the attention of logicians was again drawn to the paradoxes.

Bertrand Russell's paradox of classes

Russell discovered this paradox in June 1901. On page 75 of his book *My Philosophical Development* he says this: "I was led to this contradiction by considering Cantor's proof that there is no greatest cardinal number. I thought, in my innocence, that the number of all the things there are in the world must be the greatest possible number, and I applied his proof to this number to see what would happen. This process led me to the consideration of a very peculiar class. Thinking along the lines which had hitherto seemed inadequate, it seemed to me that a class sometimes is, and sometimes is not, a member of itself. The class of teaspoons, for example, is not another teaspoon, but the class of things that are not teaspoons, is one of the things that are not teaspoons. There seemed to be instances which are not negative: for example, the class of all classes is a class. The application of Cantor's argument led me to con-

12

sider the classes that are not members of themselves; and these, it seemed, must form a class. I asked myself whether this class is a member of itself or not. If it is a member of itself, it must possess the defining property of the class, which is to be not a member of itself. If it is not a member of itself, it must not possess the defining property of the class, and therefore must be a member of itself. Thus each alternative leads to its opposite and there is a contradiction." Further, he says that this contradiction "put an end to the logical honeymoon that I had been enjoying. I communicated the misfortune to Whitehead, who failed to console me by quoting, 'never glad confident morning again'."[9]

He says on page 147 of *The Autobiography of Bertrand Russell,* Vol. 1: "At first I supposed that I should be able to overcome the contradiction quite easily, and that probably there was some trivial error in the reasoning. Gradually however, it became clear that this was not the case. Burali-Forti had already discovered a similar contradiction, and it turned out on logical analysis that there was an affinity with the ancient Greek contradiction about Epimenides the Cretan, who said that all Cretans are liars. It seemed unworthy of a grown man to spend his time on such trivialities, but what was I to do? There was something wrong, since such contradictions were unavoidable on ordinary premisses. Trivial or not, the matter was a challenge. Throughout the latter half of 1901 I supposed the solution would be easy, but by the end of that time I had concluded that it was a big job. I therefore decided to finish *The Principles of Mathematics,* leaving the solution in abeyance. In the autumn Alys and I went back to Cambridge, as I had been invited to give two terms' lectures on mathematical logic. These lectures contained the outline of *Principia Mathematica,* but without any method of dealing with the contradictions." He says further (on page 151): "The summers of 1903 and 1904 we spent at Churt and Tilford. I made a practice of wandering about the common every night from eleven until one, by which means I came to know the three different noises made by nightjars. (Most people only know one.) I was trying hard to solve the contradictions mentioned above. Every morning I would sit down before a blank sheet of paper. Throughout the day, with a brief interval for lunch, I would stare at the blank sheet. Often when evening came it was still empty. We spent our winters in London, and during the winters I did not attempt to work, but the two summers of 1903 and 1904 remain in my mind as a period of complete intellectual deadlock. It was clear to me that I could not get on without solving the contradictions, and I was determined that no difficulty should turn me aside from the completion of *Principia Mathematica,* but it seemed quite likely that the whole of the rest of my life might be consumed in looking at that blank sheet of paper. What made it the more annoying was that the contradictions were trivial, and that my time was spent in considering matters that seemed unworthy of serious attention."[10]

Berry's paradox

This paradox was devised by G. G. Berry of the Bodleian Library and first published in 1908 by Bertrand Russell.

14

That mythical island, whose inhabitants earned a precarious living by taking in each other's washing: Lewis Carroll

The number of syllables in the English names of finite integers tends to increase as the integers grow larger, and must gradually increase indefinitely, since only a finite number of names can be made with a given finite number of syllables. Hence the names of some integers must consist of at least nineteen syllables, and among these there must be a least. Hence "the least integer not namable in fewer than nineteen syllables" must denote a definite integer; in fact, it denotes 111,777. But "the least integer not namable in fewer than nineteen syllables" is itself a name consisting of eighteen syllables; hence the least integer not namable in fewer than nineteen syllables can be named in eighteen syllables.[11]

Grelling's paradox
In 1908 the German mathematician Kurt Grelling devised this paradox, of "heterologicality": Some adjectives such as *short* and *English* apply to themselves, others such as *long* and *German* do not. Let us call those of the first group *autological,* and those of the second group *heterological.* Is the adjective heterological itself heterological? If it is, then according to the definition just given it does not apply to itself, and so it cannot be heterological. On the other hand, if it is not heterological, then according to the definition it does apply to itself, and so it must be heterological.

Self-reference can lead to vicious circularity, as in the liar paradox. Self-reference can also lead to infinity, the other pole of paradox. Here is an example of the *infinite regress* in logic:

Norman Mailer's story "The Notebook" tells of an argument between the writer and his girl friend. As they argue he jots in his notebook an idea for a story that has just come to him. It is a story about a writer who is arguing with his girl friend when he gets an idea . . .

Children sometimes tell stories like this:

It was a dark and stormy night, the rain came down in torrents, there were brigands on the mountains, and thieves, and the chief said unto Antonio: "Antonio, tell us a story." And Antonio, in fear and dread of the mighty chief, began his story: "It was a dark and stormy night, the rain came down in torrents, there were brigands on the mountains, and thieves. . . ."

Here self-reference has led into an infinite regression of storytellers and stories. This area of paradox is the meeting place between the paradoxes of self-reference and the paradoxes of infinity proper.

One might make the analogy of a mirror facing a mirror. Mirror reflects mirror, and so on to infinity. Furthermore, the archetype of a vicious circle, the ouroboros, the snake with his tail in his mouth, is sometimes known as the hieroglyph of eternity.

Chairman of a meeting of the Society of Logicians: "Before we put the motion: 'That the motion be now put,'

16

should we not first put the motion: 'That the motion: "That the motion be now put" be now put'?"

The following entry won a newspaper prize for the best piece on the topic:
"What would you most like to read on opening the morning paper?"

OUR SECOND COMPETITION
The First Prize in the second of this year's competitions goes to Mr. Arthur Robinson, whose witty entry was easily the best of those we received. His choice of what he would like to read on opening his paper was headed "Our Second Competition" and was as follows: "The First Prize in the second of this year's competitions goes to Mr. Arthur Robinson, whose witty entry was easily the best of those we received. His choice of what he would like to read on opening his paper was headed 'Our Second Competition,' but owing to paper restrictions we cannot print all of it."

This is the infinite regress and death:
"Leinbach had discovered a proof that there really is no death. It is beyond question, he had declared, that not only at the moment of drowning, but at all the moments of death of any nature, one lives over again his past life with a rapidity inconceivable to others. This remembered life must also have a last moment, and this last moment its own last moment, and so on, and hence, dying is itself eternity, and hence, in accordance with the theory of limits, one may approach death but can never reach it."

Arthur Schnitzler in "Flight into Darkness"

17

Aristotle used the regress in his famous "third man" criticism of Plato's doctrine of ideas: **If all men are alike because they have something in common with Man, the ideal and eternal archetype, how can we explain the fact that one man and Man are alike without assuming another archetype? And will not the same reasoning demand a third, fourth, and fifth archetype, and so on into the regress of more and more ideal worlds?**

A similar aversion to the infinite regress underlies Aristotle's argument, elaborated by hundreds of later philosophers, that the cosmos must have a first cause. William Paley, an eighteenth-century English theologian, put it this way: "A chain composed of an infinite number of links can no more support itself than a chain composed of a finite number of links." A finite chain does indeed require support, mathematicians were quick to point out, but in an infinite chain *every* link hangs securely on the one above.

While Eubulides of Megara got the paradoxes of self-reference off to a good start in the sixth century B.C. with the paradox of the liar, another ancient Greek, Zeno of Elea, laid the foundation of the paradoxes of infinity.

18

It is as if I were attempting to trace with the point of a pencil the shadow of the tracing pencil: Nathanael West

Zeno of Elea was probably born around 490 B.C. He seems to have written only one book, and it has been said, "What we have left of Zeno's best-known work comes, on the most hopeful view, to less than two hundred words." Since he wrote his book as "a young man," it is likely that he produced his paradoxes in the sixties, quite possibly in the early sixties, of the fifth century B.C.

Zeno made many *arguments against plurality,* perhaps forty. Two of them contain what survives in Zeno's original wording.

Zeno's first argument against plurality

If there are many (existents) they must be both so small as to have no size, and so large as to be infinite.

If there were many things, each of them would have to possess (as minimal conditions for existence) unity and self-identity. But nothing can have unity if it has size, for whatever has parts cannot be one. Hence, if there were many things, none of them could have size.

A man advertises that he could tell anyone how to make four hundred a year certain, and would do so on receipt of a shilling. To every sender he dispatched a postcard with these words: "Do as I do": Aleister Crowley

For if it (a sizeless existent) were added to another existent, it would make it (the latter) no larger. For having itself no size, it could contribute nothing by way of size when added. And thus it would follow that the thing added would be nothing. If, indeed, when something is subtracted from another, the latter is not reduced, nor again is the latter increased when the former is added to it, it is clear that what is added or subtracted is nothing.

So if many exist, each existent must have some size and bulk and some part of each must lie beyond another part of the same existent. And the same reasoning holds of the projecting part: for this too will have some size and some part of it will project. Now to say this once is as good as saying it forever. For no such part—that is, no part resulting from this continuing subdivision—will be the last nor will one part ever exist not similarly related to (that is, projecting from) another.

Thus, if there are many, they must be both small and great: on one hand, so small as to have no size; and on the other, so large as to be infinite.

Zeno's second argument against plurality

If there are many, it is necessary that they be as many as they are, neither more nor fewer. But if they are as many as they are, they must be finitely many.

If there are many, the existents must be infinitely many —for there are always other existents between existents, and again others between these. And thus the existents are infinitely many.

It is highly probable that a Zenonian original is behind this Eleatic argument:

Zeno's (?) third argument against plurality

If an existent were infinitely divisible, no contradiction should arise from the supposition that it has been divided "exhaustively" (or "through and through").

But an exhaustive division would resolve the existent into elements of zero extension. This is impossible, for no extensive magnitude could consist of extensionless elements.

On 10.6.70 the editor of the *Evening News* appeared on the television and when asked what his headline story would have been had the paper's printing not been thwarted by striking printers said that his headline would have been
THE SILENCE IN FLEET STREET

Of Zeno's *arguments against motion,* not even one line of the arguments has survived in Zeno's original wording. What we know of them derives almost exclusively from Aristotle's accounts of them in the *Physics.* We know four of them.

Zeno's racecourse, dichotomy, or bisection paradox

If a man is to walk a distance of one mile, he must first walk half the distance or one half mile, then he must walk half of what remains or one fourth mile, then again half of what remains or one eighth mile, etc. ad infinitum. An infinite series of finite distances must be successively traversed if the man is to reach the end of the mile. But an infinite series is by definition a series that cannot be exhausted, for it never comes to an end.

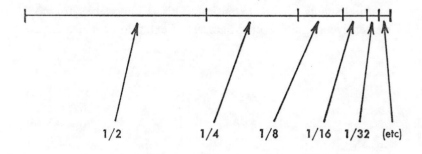

1/2   1/4   1/8   1/16 1/32 (etc)

Hence the man can never reach the end of the mile, and seeing that the same argument may be applied *mutatis mutandis* to any finite distance whatever, it is clearly impossible for motion ever to occur.

José A. Benardete has pointed out Aristotle's second formulation of the paradox:

If you count the first half of the journey and then half of what is left and so on, you would have to count an infinite series of numbers before you got to the end of the journey; which is admitted to be impossible.[12]

Zeno's Achilles and the tortoise paradox

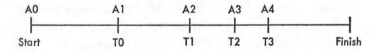

Achilles and a tortoise are to race, and the tortoise is allowed to start. Zeno says that before overtaking the tortoise Achilles must get to the place where the tortoise started from—call it T0. By the time he has got there the tortoise will have advanced to another point T1, and Achilles must now get to that point, and so on. The suggestion is that Achilles cannot overtake the tortoise or indeed catch up with him.

The handleless ax without a blade: Lichtenberg

If you turn on the light quickly enough you can see what the dark looks like

Here is a reply to Zeno, by Alan R. White:

Achilles at the shooting gallery

The shade of Achilles has given up his pursuit of the shade of the tortoise and has decided to try his luck at the shooting gallery. There the targets move from left to right across his line of vision at a slow but constant speed. Before he has time to shoot, however, the shade of Zeno insists on proffering some advice. "If you want to hit the target, then obviously you must aim at it in its present position." Achilles tries this but finds that his bullet strikes just to the left of the target. He tries a quick-firing automatic weapon but his shot, though nearer, is still to the left. Even magic bullets which travel at an incredible speed still fall, however slightly, to the left of the target moving to the right. Achilles concludes that it is as impossible to hit a moving target as to catch a moving tortoise.

At this moment the shade of Socrates appears. "Zeno has misled you. If the target moves at all, then no matter how fast your bullets and how slow the target, a shot aimed at its present position will land to the left because the target will have moved, however slightly, to the right during the

In submitting to your consideration the idea that the human mind is at its best when playing, I am myself playing, and that makes me feel that what I am saying may have in it an element of truth: J. L. Synge

time it takes your bullet to travel. You should aim for the position in which the target will be by the time your bullet has arrived; this is easily calculable from the speeds of the target and your bullet. Zeno has not proved that you cannot hit a moving target; what he has undoubtedly proved is that you cannot hit it *if* you aim at its present position."

Having put Socrates' instructions successfully to the test, Achilles begins to ponder on the advice that Zeno had given him prior to his race with the tortoise. Luckily he is able to recall the exact words: "It is necessary for the pursuer first to reach the position whence the pursued has taken off."

It immediately dawns on Achilles that Zeno's advice here is misleading in the same way as his advice at the shooting gallery. Zeno has persuaded him to try to catch the tortoise by aiming for the spot where at any given time the tortoise is. But by the time that Achilles has got there, the tortoise has moved to another, though less distant, place. By the time Achilles has reached this spot, the tortoise has moved to another, still less distant, place. However much Achilles increases his speed and however much the tortoise slows down, if Achilles always aims only for the present position of the tortoise, then the tortoise, provided he does not stop altogether, will always have reached a new position by the time Achilles has arrived at the old. Thus he will never catch the tortoise: "so that the slower must always be a bit ahead."

Zeno has cunningly persuaded Achilles to accept the mistaken belief that the only way to catch the runner in front is by forever landing on the spot from which he is now taking off. Zeno has not proved that the tortoise cannot be caught; what he has undoubtedly proved is that he cannot be caught by any series of gap closures. Adapting the advice of Socrates at the shooting gallery, the shade of Achilles challenges the shade of the tortoise to another race, aims for a calculated future position of the tortoise and catches him there.[13]

Zeno's arrow paradox

Anything which occupies a space just its own size is stationary. But in each moment of its flight an arrow can only occupy a space just its own size. Hence at each moment of its flight the arrow is not moving but stationary. But what is true of the arrow at each moment of a period is true of it throughout the period. Hence during the whole time of its flight the arrow is not moving but stationary.

The Phoenix Excrementi eat themselves, digest themselves, and give birth to themselves by evacuating their bowels: Nathanael West

Zeno's moving blocks or stadium paradox

```
        A A A A
    B  B  B  B →
         ← C C C C
```

```
        A A A A
        B B B B →
       ← C C C C
```

There are three parallel rows of bodies. All the bodies are equal in size; each row contains an equal number of them; and the bodies in each row are directly adjacent. One row (the As) is stationary. The other two (Bs and Cs) meet at the mid-point of the As and move on past each other at equal speeds, so that when the first B clears the last A in one direction the first C, moving in the opposite direction, clears the last A at the other end. Thus in the time that the first B passes half the As, from mid-point to end, it passes all the Cs. Let this time be **t**. But then if the first B takes **t** to pass n bodies (to wit, half the As) it must take not **t** but **2t** to pass 2n bodies (viz. all the Cs). So the move which takes **t** also takes **2t**; this is the alleged puzzle, and plainly it depends on disregarding the relative motions of the bodies. The Cs are moving, the As are not.

Suppose now that Zeno asks how we can specify the relative motions of the bodies. If we say that the first B can pass twice as many Cs as As in a given time, what we say entails that if in a given time it passes one C it also passes half an A. But suppose now that any A (and therefore any B or C) is an *infinitesimal* quantity. Then the B cannot pass half an A: it must pass all or nothing. And since *ex hypothesi* it *is* moving past the As it must pass a whole A in the time that it passes one C. Yet, as we set up the problem, it would pass twice as many Cs as As in a given time. So when it passes one C it also passes two Cs, and this gives Zeno his contradiction.

Zeno's paradoxes, against place, and the millet seed, conclude an exhaustive presentation of his paradoxes.

Against place
    Whatever exists is in a place.
    Therefore, place exists.
    Therefore, place is in a place, and so on ad infinitum.

The millet seed

A grain of millet falling makes no sound; how can a bushel therefore make a sound?[14]

J. A. Benardete has manufactured some elegant paradoxes on infinity in his study *Infinity*, which argues that Zeno's paradoxes have still not been "solved."

This is his formulation of the bisection paradox of Zeno:

"Put the case of a man (or a god) who walks one mile in one hour non-stop. Let him now walk only ½ mile (in ½ hour), stopping for a protracted rest of ½ hour. Resuming his walk, he now walks ¼ mile (in ¼ hour) and again pauses to rest, this time for ¼ hour. Next, he walks ⅛ mile (in ⅛ hour) and pauses to rest for ⅛ hour, &c. ad infinitum. Following that schedule of intermittent motion, he may be expected to reach the terminus of his journey, having walked (on and off) a distance of one mile, at the end of two hours. Here, then, we do in fact have an infinite succession of *actual* finite intervals, an infinite series *per se*, not merely *per accidens*. This third formulation might have been anticipated from Aristotle's own words describing Zeno's bisection paradox: 'If you count the first half of what is left and so on, you would have to count an infinite series of numbers before you got to the end of the journey; which is admitted to be impossible.'

"For how can an infinite series, i.e. a series without an end, be understood as ever coming to an end?"[15]

Benardete's string paradox

Let us take a piece of string. In the first half minute we shall form an equilateral triangle with the string; in the next quarter minute we shall employ the string to form a square; in the next eighth minute we shall form a regular pentagon; etc. ad infinitum. At the end of the minute what figure or shape will our piece of string be found to have assumed? Surely it can only be a circle. And yet how intelligible is that process? Each and every one of the polygons in our infinite series contains only a finite number of sides. There is thus a serious conceptual gap separating the circle, as the limiting case, from each and every polygon in the infinite series.[16]

Benardete's book paradox

Here is a book lying on a table. Open it. Look at the first page. Measure its thickness. It is very thick indeed for a single sheet of paper—one half inch thick. Now turn to the second page of the book. How thick is this second sheet of paper? One fourth inch thick. And the third page of the

People do not understand how that which is at variance with itself agrees with itself. There is a harmony in the bending back, as in the case of the bow and the lyre: Heraclitus

book, how thick is this third sheet of paper? One eighth inch thick, etc. ad infinitum. We are to posit not only that each page of the book is followed by an immediate successor the thickness of which is one half that of the immediately preceding page but also (and this is not unimportant) that each page is separated from page 1 by a finite number of pages. These two conditions are logically compatible: there is no certifiable contradiction in their joint assertion. But they mutually entail that there is no last page in the book. Close the book. Turn it over so that the front cover of the book is now lying face down upon the table. Now, slowly lift the back cover of the book with the aim of exposing to view the stack of pages lying beneath it. There is nothing to see. For there is no last page in the book to meet our gaze.[17]

Benardete's bullets paradox
A man is shot through the heart during the last half of a minute by A. B shoots him through the heart during the preceding one quarter minute, C during the one eighth minute before that, etc. ad infinitum. Assuming that each shot kills instantly (if the man were alive), the man must be already dead before each shot. Thus he cannot be said to have died of a bullet wound.[18]

J. A. Benardete has this to say about Zenoesque procedures:

"Waiving all metaphysics, what are the crude facts in regard to our Zeno procedure? I mean the very coarsest, shabbiest facts of all. In ½ minute let us cut a stick of wood in half. This will not be difficult provided that utopian accuracy is not required of us. In the next ¼ minute let us cut one of these pieces again in half. I think that we may succeed also in this, with the same proviso. In the next ⅛ minute we shall cut, or attempt to cut, one of these latter pieces again in half. Even if we succeed here it is a harsh, even brutal, fact that after very few cuts the minute will have elapsed, all of our efforts to discharge the Zeno procedure ad infinitum being put to nought. And not only will *we* inevitably fail in this programme, but any machine that we might build will be no more successful. Why this failure? What is its cause? Is it owing to the existence of an absolute minim (be it of space or time) that arrests our progress? Not at all. How, then, is our failure to be explained? There are many factors at work: our lack of adroitness, the bluntness of the knife, the splintering of the wood, etc. In a word, *sludge*. There is always sludge that frustrates our efforts to implement the ideal in practice, not

Unless you expect the unexpected you will never find truth, for it is hard to discover and hard to attain: Heraclitus

only in the present case but on all occasions. Sludge! It is what the Yankee calls the 'sheer cussedness' of things, that unruly, refractory element in the world that, assuming the form of mechanical friction in one case, renders the perpetual motion machine impossible and that, assuming the form of Gödel's theorem in another, renders the consistency of mathematics incapable of proof. Sludge is everywhere, it cannot be escaped, not only in the physical world but even in the realm of pure ideas. Although this principle of recalcitrance is familiar to all, it has been generally believed to be merely contingent in nature, a brute fact that has no intelligible warrant. Is it perhaps otherwise?"[19]

Just as the paradoxes of self-reference found a rebirth of interest at the end of the nineteenth century, so did the paradoxes of infinity. The mathematician Cantor came up with some paradoxical results.

Cantor's paradoxical arithmetic of infinity
Cantor defined an infinite class thus:
An infinite class has the unique property that the whole is no greater than some of its parts. He showed from his pairing of all the integers with the even integers, as in the

diagram, that **the infinity of all integers, even and odd, is equal to the infinity of even integers.** This is the fundamental paradox of all infinite classes, that there exist component parts of an infinite class which are just as great as the class itself. **The whole is no greater than some of its parts.**

1	2	3	4	5	6	7	8	etc.
↕	↕	↕	↕	↕	↕	↕	↕	
2	4	6	8	10	12	14	16	etc.

The table of one-to-one correspondence
of all numbers on one side, and even
numbers only on the other.

The German mathematician David Hilbert proposed:

Hilbert's paradox of the Grand Hotel
"Imagine a hotel with a finite number of rooms, and assume that all the rooms are occupied. A new guest arrives and asks for a room. 'Sorry'—says the proprietor—'but all the rooms are occupied.' Now let us imagine a hotel with

THE
VISUAL
ARGUMENT

tophalf
temperature
per.od
com,ma
c:l:n
end
ero
1ne
2wo
3hree
4our
5ive
s   t op!
sexxx
f_oor   clim
b

1. Visual self-reference without contradiction is as banal as verbal self-reference without contradiction. A pencil drawing of a pencil may be compared to the sentence "This sentence is in the English language." Here is a slightly stronger case of *self-reference*, in which the words are modified in order to describe themselves.

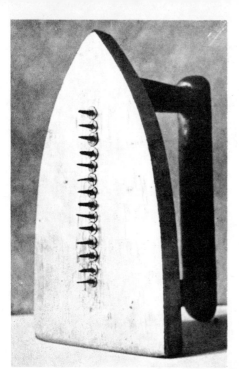

2. & 3. There is a form of visual *contradiction* without direct self-reference in some art objects. The flat iron with tacks is a blatant contradiction. Meant to run smoothly, it would stick. Meant to improve clothing, it would ruin it. However, there is a sense in which this contradiction is self-referential: in opposing tacks to the surface of the iron, Man Ray has chosen opposite ends of the same continuum, that of texture. There is nothing smoother than a smoothing-iron, and nothing rougher than tacks. Similarly hot is not the opposite of cold, they are both aspects of the same thing— temperature. The fur cup, saucer, and spoon of Méret Oppenheim contradicts our expectation of the hardness of china with the softness of fur.

Ceci n'est pas une pipe.

4. & 5. A fuller form of *self-contradiction*, though without vicious circularity, is found in "The Treachery of Images." This painting depicts a pipe, with the legend "this is not a pipe." True, it is not a pipe, you can't smoke it. False, it is a pipe, it is not a cabbage. A picture of a thing is not the thing, it represents the thing. It is and is not a pipe. The "Cloakroom Ticket" also contradicts itself.

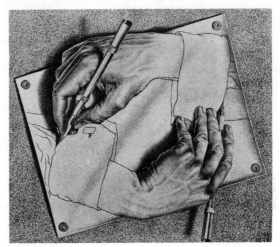

6. *Vicious circularity* is present in Escher's print "Drawing Hands." The hand is drawing the hand which is drawing the hand first mentioned. E. H. Gombrich said this of a similar drawing by Saul Steinberg: "There is a charming drawing by Saul Steinberg in which a drawing hand draws a drawing hand which draws it. We have no clue as to which is meant to be the real and which the image; each interpretation is equally probable, but neither, as such, is consistent. If proof were needed of the kinship between the language of art and the language of words, it could be found in this drawing. For the perplexing effect of this self-reference is very similar to the paradoxes beloved of philosophers: the Cretan who says all Cretans lie, or the simple blackboard with only one statement on it which runs, 'The only statement on this blackboard is untrue.'" (*Art and Illusion,* 1960, page 239.) It is interesting that the logical paradoxes attack rationalism, using the forces of reason: here Escher attacks realism, using the forces of realism.

7. "The Human Condition" of René Magritte presents what might be called the *paradox of the realistic painter*. By making the representation on the easel exactly contiguous with representation of the real world, Magritte plunges us into paradox. Magritte said of this picture: "In front of a window, as seen from the interior of a room, I placed a picture that represented precisely the portion of landscape blotted out by the picture. For instance the tree represented in the picture displaced the tree situated behind it, outside the room. For the spectator it was simultaneously inside the room, in the picture; and outside, in the real landscape, in thought." "The Human Condition" asks the question, Can reality ever be duplicated by the realistic artist? We usually answer in the negative. But, in order to ask the question, realism has been used, and we have accepted it. This is a *vicious circle*. There is an aspect of *contradiction* to this picture of Magritte's. Art, in seeking to reveal, has obscured. The realistic painter, having completed his canvas, has left us no means of deciding whether he has been completely truthful, or otherwise. In this respect he resembles the Cretan liar. He may have left out a leaf or two from the tree, or there may be no tree there at all. There is an infinity of possibility.

8. This picture shows the *realistic* painter at his paradoxical work.

9. This photo of reality confronting its representation may be one of the sources of Magritte's painting.

10. Magritte's drawing "Gigantic Days" is a paradox of vicious self-reference. It is an ambiguous picture: it may represent a woman wrestling with her own fear; it may represent a man consumed by the object of his desire.

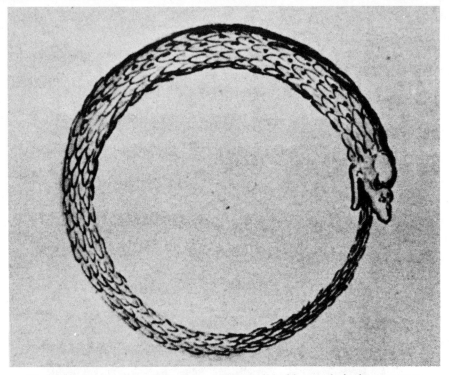

11. & 12. The ouroboros, the snake with his tail in his mouth, is the prototype of the *vicious circle*. What could be more vicious than to bite yourself, with a view, presumably, to eating yourself. Furthermore, this is impossible. Jaws can't devour jaws, the stomach can't digest itself. Surely this is the height of masochism and hunger. This task, unproductive, painful, and in the end impossible, is a good definition of paradox. Heraclitus said, "In the circle the beginning and the end are common": the ouroboros is out to prove him right. The "Endless Snake" depicts an ouroboros who has become one with himself. It has fallen into the mathematical sign for infinity, which is known as *huit clos* in French, the closed eight.

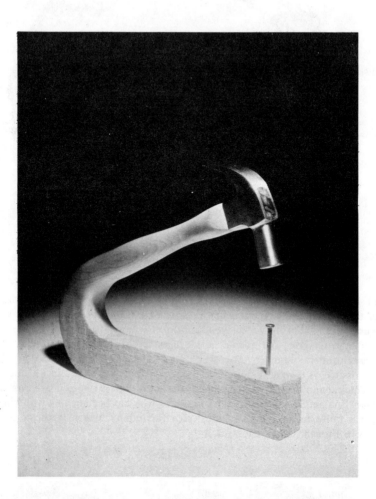

13. Malcolm Fowler's hammer nailing itself, or is it wood nailing itself, is an imaginative new version of the ouroboros.

14. The "Short Circuit" serves to illustrate the short circuit of logical paradox. The negative invites the positive, and the inert circle is complete.

15. This depicts one of the rare appearances of paradox in everyday life. It is a kind of amiable vicious circle.

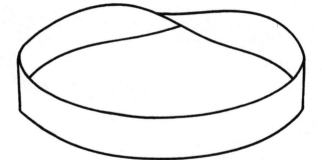

16. The Möbius strip is another example of a vicious circle. Such a circle is usually formed by taking a strip of paper, giving it a half twist, and sticking the ends of the paper together. Thus the strip turns upon itself and gobbles up one of its sides! Make one, and follow its edge. You will find it has only one edge. Similarly, it has only one side. Furthermore, if you cut it in half along a line down its middle, the result is not two bands, as one might expect, but a single larger band.

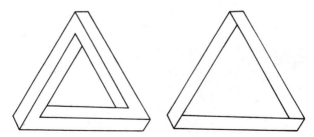

17. & 18. The Penrose triangle is itself a kind of vicious circle. It has too many sides. The Penroses derived this triangle from some of the visual contradictions in Escher's works. The triangle also seems to bear some relation to a Möbius strip with three half twists, when flattened.

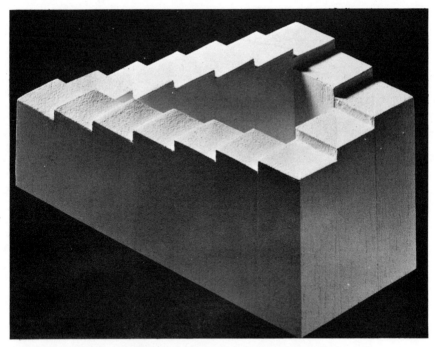

19. & 20. The Penroses also devised this circular contradiction, the Penrose stairs. It serves as a fine illustration to Heraclitus' dictum: "The way up and the way down are one and the same."

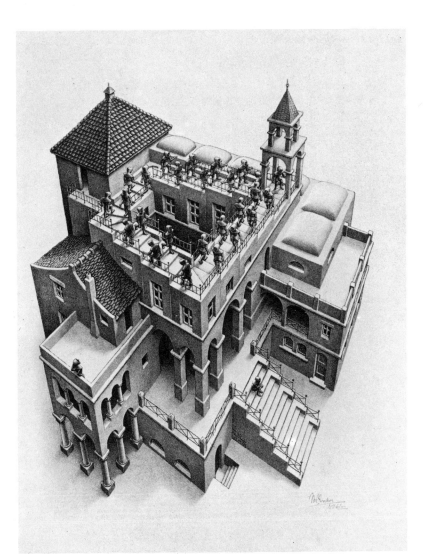

21. As the Penroses drew on the work of Escher to invent their triangle and stairs, so then did Escher draw on their work, and, for instance, made this print. The Penroses are scientists, and Escher is an artist. (C. P. Snow will be pleased!) Samuel Butler seems appropriate to this image: "We say 'everything has a beginning.' This is one side of the matter. There is another, according to which nothing has a beginning. According to this, beginnings and endings are but as it were steps cut in a slope of ice without which we could not climb it. They are for convenience, and the hardness of men's hearts makes an idol of classification, but they are nothing apart from our sense of our own convenience."

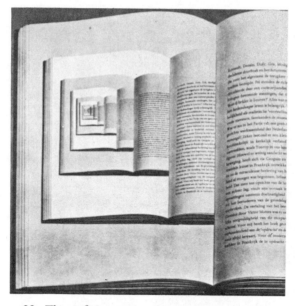

22. The *infinite regress* is sometimes met in reality, when a mirror on a wall faces another on the opposite wall, or when one is in a mirrored room. It is also sometimes met on cornflake packages which choose to represent a family consuming cornflakes from a package on which is represented a family, etc.

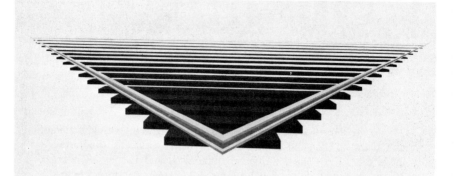

23. The *actual infinite* is rarely met with visually, owing to the workings of perspective, which puts vanishing points at some mere miles distant. Infinity is farther away than this. This is an attempt to represent infinity from the other end.

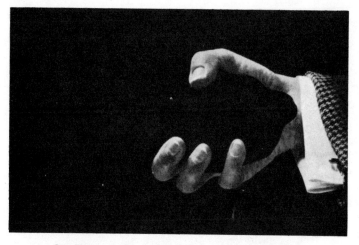

24. The *paradox of nothing* is represented here.

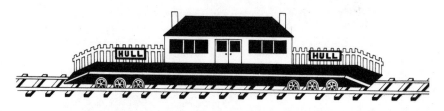

25. A delightful example of paradox in everyday life is presented to the senses when, in a train, a train opposite moves off and one has the sensation of moving backward. Here is a quote from Tom Stoppard's play *Jumpers,* first performed in 1972:

GEORGE: A remarkable number of apparently intelligent people are baffled by the fact that a different group of apparently intelligent people profess to a knowledge of God when common sense tells *them*—the first group of apparently intelligent people—that knowledge is only a possibility in matters that can be demonstrated to be true or false, such as that the Bristol train leaves from Paddington. And yet these same apparently intelligent people, who in extreme cases will not even admit that the Bristol train left from Paddington yesterday—which might be a malicious report or a collective trick of memory—nor that it will leave from there tomorrow—for nothing is certain—and will only agree that it did so today if they were actually there when it left—and even then only on the understanding that all the observable phenomena associated with the train leaving Paddington could equally well be accounted for by Paddington leaving the train. (Tom Stoppard, *Jumpers,* London, 1972, page 88.)

26. A final example of paradox in everyday life.

an infinite number of rooms, and all the rooms are occupied. To this hotel, too, comes a new guest and asks for a room. 'But of course!'—exclaims the proprietor, and he moves the person previously occupying room N1 into room N2, the person from room N2 into room N3, the person from room N3 into room N4, and so on . . . And the new customer receives room N1, which became free as the result of these transpositions.

"Let us imagine now a hotel with an infinite number of rooms, all taken up, and an infinite number of new guests who come in and ask for rooms.

"'Certainly, gentlemen,' says the proprietor, 'just wait a minute.' He moves the occupant N1 into N2, the occupant of N2 into N4, the occupant of N3 into N6, and so on, and so on . . .

"Now all odd-numbered rooms become free and the infinity of new guests can easily be accommodated in them."

P. E. B. Jourdain describes the difficulties of a man with a Cantorian income:

"Now, if a man had an unlimited income, it is an im-

A good egg is an egg-shaped egg. Once an egg begins to break with its true shape, it is only a matter of time before it acquires wings and feathers. And along that road, make no mistake about it, lie the flying egg, the mating egg, and—ultimate absurdity—the egg-laying egg: N. F. Simpson

mediate inference that, however low income-tax may be, he would have to pay annually to the Exchequer of his nation a sum equal in value to his whole income. Further, if his income was derived from a capital invested at a finite rate of interest (as is usual), the annual payments of income-tax would each be equal in value to the man's whole capital. If, then, the man with an unlimited income chose to be discontented, he would be sure of a sympathetic audience among philosophers and business acquaintances; but discontent could not last long, for the thought of the difficulties he was putting in the way of the Chancellor of the Exchequer, who would find the drawing up of his budget most puzzling, would be amusing. Again, the discovery that, after paying an infinite income-tax, the income would be quite undiminished, would obviously afford satisfaction, though perhaps the satisfaction might be mixed with a slight uneasiness as to any action the Commissioners of Income-Tax might take in view of this fact."[20]

Cantor showed that there are many more points on a line than there are integers or fractional numbers.

He also showed that the number of all ordinary arithmetical fractions like 3/7 or 735/8 is the same as the number of all integers.

Cantor showed that there is the same number of points in lines one inch, one foot, or one mile long. Look at the illustration, which compares the number of points on two

lines AB and AC of different lengths. To establish the one-
to-one correspondence between the points of these two
lines we draw through each point on AB a line parallel to
BC, and pair the points of intersections as for example D
and D1, E and E1, F and F1, etc. Each point on AB has
a corresponding point on AC and vice versa; thus the two
infinities of points are equal.

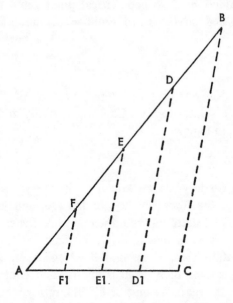

Cantor further showed that **the number of all points on a
plane is equal to the number of all points on a line.**

In a similar way he showed that **the infinity of all points**

within a cube is the same as the infinity of points within a square or on a line.

But the number of all geometric points, though larger than the number of all integers and fractional numbers, is not the largest one known to mathematicians. In fact it was found that **the variety of all possible curves, including those of most unusual shapes, has a larger membership than the collection of all geometrical points, and thus has to be described as the third number of the infinite sequence.**

Bertrand Russell proposed **the paradox of Tristram Shandy** which relates to both Cantorian infinity and the infinite regress in logic.

"Tristram Shandy, as we know, took two years writing the history of the first two days of his life, and lamented that, at this rate, material would accumulate faster than he could deal with it, so that he could never come to an end. Now I maintain that, if he had lived for ever, and not wearied of his task, then, even if his life had continued as eventfully as it began, no part of his biography would have remained unwritten."

"My friend Jones will vouch for me." "How do we know that he can be trusted?" "Oh, I assure you he can"

Recently philosophers of science have considered new paradoxes of infinity, called supertasks. For instance, imagine a lamp (called the Thomson lamp, after James F. Thomson, who first wrote about it) that is turned off and on by a push-button switch. Starting at zero time, the lamp is on for one half minute, then it is off for one quarter minute, then on for one eighth minute, and so on. Since the sum of this halving series, $\frac{1}{2}+\frac{1}{4}+\frac{1}{8}+$ . . . is 1, at the end of one minute the switch will have been moved an infinite number of times. Will the lamp be on or off?

Similarly, Max Black has invited consideration of several processes involving infinite transfers of marbles.

Infinity machine Alpha

Let us suppose that upon our left a narrow tray stretches into the distance as far as the most powerful telescope can follow; and that this tray or slot is full of marbles. Here, at the middle, where the line of marbles begins, there stands a kind of mechanical scoop; and to the right, a second, but empty tray, stretching away into the distance beyond the farthest reach of vision. Now the machine is started. During the first minute of its operation, it seizes a marble from the left and transfers it to the empty tray on the right; then it rests a minute. In the next half minute the machine seizes a second marble on the left, transfers it, and rests half a minute. The third marble is moved in a quarter of a minute, with a corresponding pause; the next in one

The biter bit

eighth of a minute; and so until the movements are so fast that all we can see is a gray blur. But at the end of exactly four minutes the machine comes to a halt, and now the left-hand tray that was full seems to be empty, while the right-hand tray that was empty seems full of marbles.[21]

Infinity machine Beta

Let there be only *one* marble in the left-hand tray to begin with, and let some device always return *that same marble* during the time at which the machine is resting. From the standpoint of the machine, as it were, the task has not changed. Imagine Alpha and Beta set to work side by side on their respective tasks: every time the one moves, so does the other; if one succeeds in its task, so must the other; and if it is impossible for either to succeed, it is impossible for *each*. [22]

Infinity machine Gamma

Works like Beta but from *right to left*. Let it be arranged that no sooner does Beta move the marble from left to right than Gamma moves it back again. The successive working periods and pauses are then equal in length to those of Beta, except that Gamma is working while Beta is resting, and vice versa. The task of Gamma, moreover, is exactly parallel to that of Beta, that is, to transfer the marble an infinite number of times from one side to the other.[23]

The Queen had been called a great many things, but nobody had ever said she was proud; this was her pride: Ronald Firbank

40

A paradox which has had some currency from 1943 onward, and which is first mentioned in print in 1948, is the **surprise inspection paradox**. It has also been known as the **hangman**, the **class A blackout**, the **unexpected egg**, the **senior sneak week**, the **prediction paradox**, and the **unexpected examination**. Since this paradox is so recent, the literature on it is of a finite quantity and readily available. We have studied most of the material and present a selection of it here. It is a fascinating example of the logicophilosophical community at work. The author of this paradox is not known, but D. J. O'Connor first formulates the paradox in print in his article "Pragmatic Paradoxes" in the philosophical quarterly *Mind,* 1948:

"**The military commander of a certain camp announces on a Saturday evening that during the following week there will be a 'Class A Blackout.' The date and time of the exercise are not prescribed because a 'Class A Blackout' is defined in the announcement as an exercise which the participants cannot know is going to take place prior to 6.00 p.m. on the evening in which it occurs. It is easy to**

41

see that it follows from the announcement of this definition that the exercise cannot take place at all. It cannot take place on Saturday because if it has not occurred on one of the first six days of the week it must occur on the last. And the fact that the participants can know this violates the condition which defines it. Similarly, because it cannot take place on Saturday, it cannot take place on Friday either, because when Saturday is eliminated Friday is the last available day and is, therefore, invalidated for the same reason as Saturday. And by similar arguments, Thursday, Wednesday, etc., back to Sunday are eliminated in turn, so that the exercise cannot take place at all."[24]

O'Connor remarks: "Now though there is an obvious fault of definition in this case, the fault is not a fault of logic in the sense that the definition is formally self-contradictory. It is merely *pragmatically* self-refuting. The conditions of the action are defined in such a way that their publication entails that the action can never be carried out." He goes on to say that "it is rather a frivolous example."

P. J. Alexander in his article "Pragmatic Paradoxes," in *Mind*, 1950, suggests:

"Professor O'Connor's statement, which can be abbreviated to read 'A "Class A Blackout" will be carried out next week' *ought* for completeness, to read 'If the conditions of a "Class A Blackout" can be realised, a "Class A Blackout" will be carried out next week.'"

M. Scriven in his article "Paradoxical Announcements," in *Mind*, 1951, begins:

"A new and powerful paradox has come to light."

And he says of O'Connor's remarks about the paradox:

"It is not frivolous, for a reason which has escaped him. Suppose that the Commanding Officer arranges for a blackout to take place during the period covered by the announcement. Clearly the date of its occurrence cannot be forecast from the announcement. So it will by definition be a 'Class A Blackout,' and he will be entirely justified in his announcement that a 'Class A Blackout' would take place during this period. Yet, in some sense 'the exercise cannot take place at all.' It appears that the logical gadget which established this conclusion has somehow short-circuited. I think this flavour of logic refuted by the world makes the paradox rather fascinating. The logician goes pathetically through the motions that have always worked the spell before, but somehow the monster, Reality, has missed the point and advances still."

Scriven asks us to:

"Consider next **the inquisitor who points at two boxes on his desk numbered '1' and '2' and says 'In one of these boxes is an unexpected egg. You may open them only in the order of their numbers. Which box contains the unexpected egg?'** We should not be clear what he meant by an unexpected egg. To begin with it can't be completely unexpected since we know it is in one of two boxes. And then we might see that if there were no egg in box number one, there would be no unexpectedness at all about its unexpectedness in box two. This makes us feel that it must be in box one; yet if it must be there how can it be unexpected? It looks as if there cannot be an unexpected egg there at all. Puzzled, we might say to the inquisitor 'Look, your remark doesn't make good sense when announced to me, for I can show from it that there cannot be an unexpected egg in either box.' He replies 'Surely the matter is simple enough; there *is* an egg in one of the two boxes and you can't argue it away, nor have you by argument decided in which box it is. Ergo, it is an unexpected egg.' And now we have him. For if this is what he means we can argue as follows. 'If the egg is not in box one, we should know before opening the second lid that it was in box two, and it would not be unexpected. So the only possibility which might make you right, is that the egg is in box one. Yet since we shall expect to find the egg there, it will not be unexpected; in fact, the egg cannot be unexpected, so you are wrong. We do *not* have to show in which box the egg reposes in order to show that it is not unexpected, but only that it cannot be in either and be unexpected. We were puzzled at first because it seemed the egg had some magic property that caused it to vanish whenever we had deduced its whereabouts. But now you tell us that there is a real egg in one of the boxes and you go on wrongly to claim that it will not be unexpected. True, it may be expected wrongly but only if your own statement was wrong. There is something very queer about the statement "There is an unexpected egg in one box." It suggests, or can be taken to suggest, one state of affairs: the presence of a special kind of egg. But we find that this isn't a special kind of egg in the way that speckled, double yolked, or Easter eggs are special. Not at all: unexpected eggs, for one thing, may be expected eggs at the same time

44

(with respect to the conditions of some other problem and problem-solver). Yet the argument proceeds as though they were eggs with some observable peculiarity, and when (on that assumption) we have deduced their whereabouts, the prize is magically spirited away. The argument which works so well with addled or ostrich eggs whose presence is asserted in one of the boxes, will not do for unexpected eggs (or, if you like, the assertion won't do), because neither of the possible alternatives, (1) there must be an unexpected egg in box one, or (2) there must be an unexpected egg in box two, is sensible if the unexpectedness applies to the person to whom the alternatives are presented. Since these statements are not in themselves sensible, it is not sensible to talk of ruling them out. Nor sensible to make a statement which is equivalent to a disjunction of such alternatives.'"

In *Scientific American,* 1963, Martin Gardner proposed a variation on this paradox of Scriven's:

"**Imagine that you have before you 10 boxes labeled from 1 to 10. While your back is turned, a friend conceals an egg in one of the boxes. You turn around. 'I want you to open these boxes one at a time,' he tells you, 'in serial order. Inside one of them I guarantee that you will find an unexpected egg. By "unexpected" I mean that you will not be able to deduce which box it is in before you open the box and see it.'**"

Assuming that your friend is absolutely trustworthy in all his statements, can his prediction be fulfilled? Apparently not. He obviously will not put the egg in box 10 because after you have found the first nine boxes empty you will be able to deduce with certainty that the egg is in the only remaining box. This would contradict your friend's statement. Box 10 is out. Now consider the situation that would arise if he were so foolish as to put the egg in box 9. You would find the first eight boxes empty. Only 9 and 10 remain. The egg cannot be in box 10. Ergo it must be in 9. You open 9. Sure enough, there it is. Clearly it is an *expected* egg, and so your friend is again proved wrong. Box 9 is out. But now you have started on your inexorable slide into unreality. Box 8 can be ruled out by precisely the same logical argument, and similarly boxes 7, 6, 5, 4, 3, 2, and 1. Confident that all 10 boxes are empty, you start to open them. What have we here in box 5? A totally unexpected egg! Your friend's prediction is fulfilled after all. Where did your reasoning go wrong?"

Gardner goes on:
"To sharpen the paradox still more, we can consider it in a third form, one that can be called the paradox of the unexpected spade. **Imagine that you are sitting at a card table opposite a friend who shows you that he holds in his hand the 13 spades. He shuffles them, fans them with the faces toward him and deals a single card face down on the table. You are asked to name slowly the 13 spades, starting with the ace and ending with the king. Each time you fail to name the card on the table he will say 'No.' When you name the card correctly, he will say 'Yes.' 'I'll wager a thousand dollars against a dime,' he says, 'that you will not be able to deduce the name of this card before I respond with "Yes."'**

46

"Assuming that your friend will do his best not to lose his money, is it possible that he placed the king of spades on the table? Obviously not. After you have named the first 12 spades, only the king will remain. You will be able to deduce the card's identity with complete confidence. Can it be the queen? No, because after you have named the jack only the king and queen remain. It cannot be the king, so it must be the queen. Again, your correct deduction would win you $1,000. The same reasoning rules out all the remaining cards. Regardless of what card it is, you should be able to deduce its name in advance. The logic seems airtight. Yet it is equally obvious, as you stare at the back of the card, that you have not the foggiest notion what spade it is!"

Gardner continues:

"Even if the paradox is simplified by reducing it to two days, two boxes, two cards, something highly peculiar continues to trouble the situation. **Suppose your friend holds only the ace and deuce of spades. It is true that you will be able to collect your bet if the card is the deuce. Once you have named the ace and it has been eliminated you will be able to say: 'I deduce that it's the deuce.'** This deduction rests, of course, on the truth of the statement 'The card before me is either the ace or the deuce of spades.' (It is assumed by everybody that there *is* an egg in a box, that the cards *are* the cards designated.) This is as strong a deduction as mortal man can ever make a fact of nature. You have, therefore, the strongest possible claim to the $1,000. Suppose, however, your friend puts down the ace of spades.

Cannot you deduce at the outset that the card is the ace? Surely he would not risk his $1,000 by putting down the deuce. Therefore it *must* be the ace. You state your conviction that it is. He says 'Yes.' Can you legitimately claim to have won the bet? Curiously, you cannot, and here we touch on the heart of the mystery. Your deduction rested only on the premise that the card was either the ace or the deuce. The card is not the ace; therefore it is the deuce. But now your deduction rests on the same premise as before plus an additional one, namely on the assumption that he will do all he can to avoid paying you $1,000. But if it is possible for you to deduce that the card is the ace, he will lose his money just as surely as if he put down the deuce. Since he loses it either way, he has no rational basis for picking one card rather than the other. Once you realize this your deduction that the card is the ace takes an extremely shaky character. It is true that you would be wise to bet that it is the ace, because it probably is, but to win the bet you have to do more than that: you have to prove that you have deduced the card with iron logic. This you cannot do.

"You are, in fact, caught up in a vicious circle of contradictions. First you assume that his prediction will be fulfilled. On this basis you deduce that the card on the table is the ace. But if it is the ace, his prediction is falsified. If his prediction cannot be trusted, you are left without a rational basis for deducing the name of the card. And if you cannot deduce the name of the card, his prediction will certainly be confirmed. Now you are right back where you started. The

48

whole circle begins again. In this respect the situation is
analogous to the vicious circularity involved in Jourdain's
paradox of the card, on one side of which is the sentence
'the statement on the other side of this card is true' and on
the other side of which is the sentence 'the statement on the
other side of this card is false.' "

Paul Weiss in his article in *Mind,* 1952, asks:
"I hope Mr. O'Connor will not mind my giving his paradox the new and somewhat more appropriate name of 'the
prediction paradox.' I hope too, he will not mind my using
a different illustration of a more practical, poignant and
permanent interest than his, and that he will excuse my re-
fining his formulation a little. (Mr. O'Connor so states the
paradox that it is possible for the announcement to be re-
scinded, with the consequence that the non-occurrence of
the blackout rather than its occurrence could be predicted.)

"A headmaster says, 'It is an unbreakable rule in this
school that there be an examination on an unexpected day.'
The students argue that the examination cannot be given
on the last day of the school year, for if it had not been
given until then, it could be given only on that day and
would then be no longer unexpected. Nor, say they, can
it be given on the next to last day, for with the last day
eliminated, the next to the last day will be the last, so that
the previous argument holds, and so on and so on. Either
the headmaster gives the examination on an unexpected
day or he does not give it at all. In either case he will break

49

an unbreakable rule; in either case he must fail to give an examination on an unexpected day."

Weiss goes on to name five cases:

"1. On the last day of the term, the headmaster says, 'Oh, by the way, I forgot to tell you about an unbreakable rule in this school. We must have an examination on a previously unexpected day. Please take out your pencils and write down and answer the following questions.' There is no doubt but that the day and the examination will be totally unexpected. Instead of prohibiting the giving of the examination, the announcement will require the examination, to the consternation of totally unprepared boys. If we wish to produce a paradox we must suppose that the announcement be made not on the last day but on some other. This points up the fact that the paradox is a function, not of the announcement, but of the relation of the announcement to the announced occurrence.

"2. The headmaster, on some day of the term other than the last, announces: 'There is an unbreakable rule that we must have an examination on a previously unexpected day, and this is it.' Once again the day will be unexpected; once again there will be no paradox. If we wish to produce a paradox we must insist that the announcement be made before the day on which the examination is given. The first case discussed above is evidently a special case of this; the general rule is not that the announcement must be made on a day before the last, but that it must be made on a day before the examination is given."

Weiss asks: "Can we expect the announcing of an announcement which says that it will be announced unexpectedly?" And answers: "It seems evident that we have no grounds in an announcement for an expectation that the announcement will be announced in the particular way or time in which it is announced. There is something unexpected in the act of announcing, just as surely as there is something unexpectable in the occurrence of the events covered by the announcement."

Weiss makes three further points:
"3. The headmaster makes his statement in the evening, two days before the last. It is then true that 'the examination will be given the next day or the day after'; it will not then be true that 'it will be given the next day' or true that 'it will be given on the last day.' There is as yet no distinct next day or day after on which the examination could be given. If the examination is not given the next day, when that day comes around, there will, of course, be no alternative left but that of the last day. It is no surprise then that if we think of ourselves as at the last day, as the paradox requires, and then proceed to eliminate that day, we will find there is no day left on which the examination could be given, the other days having already been eliminated in the act of coming to the last day. When the announcement is made it is not predictable which of two days will be the day on which the examination will be given, but once we have eliminated the first of these days in fact or in imagination, the examination must occur on the second day. But until the days have been distinguished they are not alterna-

tives, excluding one another. He who supposes that they are, and therefore argues that the examination cannot be given, will find to his surprise that the examination is given at a totally unexpected time.

"4. Suppose the examination had not been given by the time the last day came around. Suppose too, that a student had paid no attention to the announcement when it was made some time previous to the last day. Suppose, finally, that the student suddenly remembered the announcement that day. The examination will certainly come on an unexpected day for him, though there is, in fact, only one day on which it could occur. This conclusion does not go counter to our observation above. A student to whom the announcement was not communicated (because of his inattention or otherwise) is confronted with the possibility not of 'examination today or not today' but with the possibility 'examination or no examination today.' He does not know, before he remembers the announcement, whether an examination will be given or whether an examination will not be given. In remembering the announcement he eliminates, as no longer pertinent to him, the alternative 'no examination today.' The elimination is unpredictable; it cannot be determined by a consideration of the range of possibility open to him. When, though, the alternative of 'no examination today' has been eliminated by him, there is, of course, no alternative left but that of 'examination today.' What will then be unpredictable will be the exact time or nature of the examination. This he can know when he is in the actual presence of the examination, not before.

"When and as the examination occurs it is not unexpected; it is unexpected only before it occurs. Or, if by 'examination' we mean to represent a possibility of long or short, fair or unfair, etc., examination, an examination of some sort will be rightly expected but one could not predict its length or fairness—prediction being understood to be grounded in present data or to infer, with warrant, what this entails."

Weiss concludes his five points:
"5. If the headmaster were to make his statement before school opened, the students would have to be prepared for an examination on any day at all. That examination will occur some time in school term. But they cannot know, they cannot predict, they cannot rightly expect the day on which it will occur. If the examination is not given by the time the last day comes around, the examination will have to be given on that last day. That day will have been unexpected all along. When it comes around it will, of course, no longer be an unexpected day, for what is now present is no longer unexpected. But the last day cannot be dislocated from the other days at the time the announcement is made, except by a kind of theoretical anticipation of actual history, and thus by moving away from the announcement of a possibility to that state of affairs where possibilities are specified and distinguished one after the other. The announcement tells us that some one day will be selected as the day of the examination. Whatever one it be, it will be unexpected, so far as we view it from the standpoint of the announcement; it will

be expectable so far as we have eliminated the others and thus made it distinct from them—a status it does not have in the announcement."

In his piece in *Mind*, 1953, W. V. O. Quine, having discussed the paradox in a man-to-be-hanged form, says:

"K's fallacy may be brought into stronger relief by taking n as 1 and restoring the hanging motif. The judge tells K on Sunday afternoon that he, K, will be hanged the following noon and will remain ignorant of the fact till the intervening morning. It would be like K to protest at this point that the judge was contradicting himself. And it would be like the hangman to intrude upon K's complacency at 11.55 next morning, thus showing that the judge had said nothing more self-contradictory than the simple truth. If K had reasoned correctly, Sunday afternoon, he would have reasoned as follows. 'We must distinguish four cases: first, that I shall be hanged tomorrow noon and I know it now (but I do not); second, that I shall be unhanged tomorrow noon and know it now (but I do not); third, that I shall be unhanged tomorrow noon and do not know it now. The latter two alternatives are the open possibilities, and the last of all would fulfill the decree. Rather than charging the judge with self-contradiction, therefore, let me suspend judgement and hope for the best.'"

R. Shaw, in his article in *Mind*, 1958, suggests the following rules for the school where the unexpected exam is to take place:

"Rule 1: An examination will take place on one day of next term.

"Rule 2: The examination will be unexpected, in the sense that it will take place on such a day that on the previous evening it will not be possible for the pupils to deduce *from Rule 1* that the examination will take place on the morrow.

"The last day of term is then ruled out as a possible day for the examination, since it would violate Rule 2. However, *any other choice for the day of the examination would satisfy both Rule 1 and Rule 2.* Thus in this case, no paradox results; the rules are self consistent and are satisfied by any choice of day except the last day of term.

"Suppose we now add a third rule:
"Rule 3: The examination will take place on such a day that on the previous evening it will not be possible for the pupils to deduce *from Rules 1 and 2* that the examination will take place on the morrow.

"Then, by Rule 2, the last day of term is again not a possible day, but now the next to last day is ruled out also. For if no examination had taken place when there were only two days of term left, then the pupils could deduce from Rule 1 that the examination would take place on one of these two days, and from Rule 2 that it would not take place on the last day, and hence from Rules 1 and 2 that it would take place on the morrow. This deduction would violate Rule 3, and so the last two days are not possible days for the examination. However, any other choice of day would satisfy all three rules, and so no paradox results, provided the term lasts more than two days."

"When you say 'hill,' " the Queen interrupted, "*I* could show you hills, in comparison with which you'd call that a valley": Lewis Carroll

Shaw concludes:

"The original paradox arose by taking in addition to Rule 1 (an examination will take place on one day of next term) only the following rule:

"Rule 2*: The examination will take place on such a day that on the previous evening the pupils will not be able to deduce from Rules 1 and 2* that the examination will take place on the morrow. It is clear that the origin of the paradox lies in the self-referring nature of Rule 2*."

David Kaplan and Richard Montague in their article "A Paradox Regained" in the *Notre Dame Journal of Formal Logic,* 1960, are not so keen to dispose of the paradox:

"Treatments of this paradox have for the most part proceeded by explaining it away, that is, by offering formulations which can be shown not to be paradoxical. We feel, that the interesting problem in this domain is of a quite different character; it is to discover an exact formulation of the puzzle which is genuinely paradoxical. The Hangman might then take a place beside the Liar and the Richard paradox, and not unthinkably, lead like them to important technical progress" (in logic).

In his article in *Mind,* 1961, entitled "Unexpected Examinations and Unprovable Statements," G. C. Nerlich says this:

"The pupils' argument consists of stages, and at the end of each stage they get the *negation* of a statement of the

56

form 'examination on——day.' So that all they can deduce in the argument is that none of the days is a day for which the examination can have been arranged. But then, if they take it as proved that no unexpected examination can be set, any examination which *is* set will find them unprepared, and so it will be unexpected. That is, any day excluded in the argument satisfies this description: 'a day such that it is not possible to deduce from the head's statement, at any time prior to the day, that the examination *has* been arranged for this day.' Since all we get in the argument are statements which are *negations* of dates for the examination, we never get one of the right form to falsify the head's statement. And once we get to the position where we have deduced the negation of each of the alternatives set out in the remark 'an examination has been arranged for one of the five days of week W,' it is obvious that there is no further deduction to be carried on. We have gone as far as we can go, and are still without the examination date."

Nerlich continues:
"In so far as it is about provability, this is a little like the state of affairs in Gödel's theorem. (Not in so far as it involves self-reference, since that is not central to our problem at all.) Gödel proves that the sentence G is a proper sentence. But what G says is that G is not provable, i.e. it says this of itself. Gödel says that if this logical system is to be consistent then G must be undecidable, for if we prove G, then that proves that G is provable, i.e. G is not provable is provable, a contradiction again. So that if the system is consistent then it cannot be complete too, for if either G

or its negation is provable, we get a contradiction. Our system is rather like this too."

Nerlich concludes:
"I may know (because I have seen) which cards are held in a player's hand. If he says that he will play a certain one unexpectedly, and leave that card till last, then I have a right to discount his claim to play it unexpectedly. Though it may be worth noticing here, that since he appears to have contradicted himself, I have no kind of assurance that he will play the card at all. For *he* said he would play it, not anyone else, and his assertions no longer seem to be comprehensible. In the case we have been considering all along, one person is the source of all we know, and when our only source of information seems to impeach itself, then we do not know what to make of it. That is precisely what this particular source of our knowledge wants to achieve. One way of saying nothing is to contradict yourself. And if you manage to contradict yourself by saying that you are saying nothing, then you do not, in the end, contradict yourself at all. You *can* eat your cake, and have it too."

Martin Gardner had noted something similar, in his article previously mentioned:

"We can reduce the paradox to its essence by taking a cue from Scriven. Suppose a man says to his wife: 'My dear, I'm going to surprise you on your birthday tomorrow by giving you a completely unexpected gift. You have no way of

guessing what it is. It is that gold bracelet you saw last week in Tiffany's window.'

"What is the poor wife to make of this? She knows her husband to be truthful. He always keeps his promises. But if he does give her the gold bracelet, it will not be a surprise. This would falsify his prediction. And if his prediction is unsound, what *can* she deduce? Perhaps he will keep his word about giving her the bracelet but violate his word that the gift will be unexpected. On the other hand, he may keep his word about the surprise but violate it about the bracelet and give her instead, say, a new vacuum cleaner. Because of the self-refuting character of her husband's statement, she has no rational basis for expecting the gold bracelet. It is easy to guess what happens. On her birthday she is surprised to receive a logically unexpected bracelet.

"*He* knew all along that he could and would keep his word. *She* could not know this until after the event. A statement that yesterday appeared to be nonsense, that plunged her into an endless whirlpool of logical contradictions, has today suddenly been made perfectly true and non-contradictory by the appearance of the gold bracelet. Here in the starkest possible form is the queer verbal magic that gives to the paradoxes their bewildering, head-splitting charm."

To conclude our study of the surprise inspection, here are two remarks from J. Schoenberg, from *Mind*, 1966.

Chuang Tzu dreamt he was a butterfly and did not know, when he awoke, if he was a man who had dreamt he was a butterfly or a butterfly who now dreamt he was a man

"Suppose it is Monday morning, just before the school day begins. The six days of the school week are ahead. How can the students know at that time that each one of the days in turn must be the day and therefore not be the day? It is clear that they have reached this conclusion only by assuming that if they were unexamined on Friday, then Thursday, then Wednesday, etc., they would be able to accumulate this knowledge.

"I would like to conclude with a brief comment on Mr. Nerlich's treatment of this paradox, for it seems to me to illustrate the impossibility of reaching any positive conclusions without going beyond the description itself. As I understand his article, he accepts the argument adduced in the paradox, and then carries it further. He points out that if all the days are negated as possible days for the event, then there are no grounds for assuming that it will occur, so that whenever it does occur it comes as a complete surprise. It might also be argued, perhaps, that if all the days are negated, then all the days are the same in so far as their probability of being the day of the examination. But a difficulty appears here, for this turning of the argument makes the possibility of the event follow from the previously established negation. The result is that Saturday becomes a possible day, and this would seem to be a fatal result. Because the impossibility of Saturday was accepted at the beginning as being a valid inference from the defined conditions of the event, and, as such, was accepted as the original premise upon which the whole argument rests. To negate it, is to ne-

"I'm so glad I don't like asparagus," said the small girl to a sympathetic friend. "Because, if I did, I should have to eat it—and I can't bear it!": Lewis Carroll

gate the point of departure of the argument. So that this constitutes a reduction ad absurdum, and if the reasoning leading to it were valid, this could only prove that the defined conditions led to a contradiction. That is, Saturday would be both impossible and possible. Thus the original paradox is transformed, but not resolved."

If the rich could hire other people to die for them, the poor could make a wonderful living: Yiddish proverb

E. V. Milner's **paradox of Dives and Lazarus** bears a strong resemblance to the prediction paradox. He speaks of that surprise inspection up there in the sky.

"I have named this paradox after the characters in the New Testament parable (St. Luke, Chapter 16). In this parable a rich man Dives, and Lazarus, a beggar at his gate, both die. The former is consigned forthwith to Hell, but the beggar is received into 'Abraham's bosom.' The rich man, seeing this abrupt reversal of their respective earthly lots, pleads with Abraham for mercy. Abraham, however, refuses this, saying, 'Son, remember that thou in thy lifetime receivedst thy good things, and likewise Lazarus evil things; but now he is comforted and thou are tormented.' As a last resort the rich man then implores Abraham to send Lazarus to warn 'his five brethren' of what lay in store for them, 'lest they also come into this place of torment.' But this plea was also rejected: 'If they hear not Moses and the prophets, neither will they be persuaded though one rose from the dead.'

"Suppose, however, that this last request of Dives had been granted; suppose, in fact, that some means were found to convince the living, whether rich men or beggars, that 'justice would be done' in a future life, then, it seems to me, an interesting paradox would emerge. For if I *knew* that the unhappiness which I suffer in this world would be recompensed by eternal bliss in the next world, then I should be happy in *this* world. But being happy in this world I should fail to qualify, so to speak, for happiness in the next world. Therefore, if there were such a recompense awaiting me, its existence would seem to entail that I should at least be not wholly convinced of its existence. Put epigrammatically, it would appear that the proposition 'Justice will be done' can only be true for one who believes it to be false. For one who believes it to be true, justice is being done already."[25]

The *negation* to which Miss Schoenberg refers is a rich source of paradox. This is Kafka in his *Parables:*

Now the Sirens have a still more fatal weapon than their song, namely their silence. And though admittedly such a thing has never happened, still it is conceivable that some-one might possibly have escaped from their singing; but from their silence certainly never.

And this is the medieval writer Passerat:

Nothing is richer than precious stones and than gold; nothing is finer than adamant, nothing nobler than the blood of kings; nothing is sacred in wars; nothing is higher than heaven; nothing is lower than hell, or more glorious than virtue.

A red rose absorbs all colours but red; red is therefore the one colour that it is not: Aleister Crowley

And this is the mystic Lao Tzu:

Thirty spokes share one hub. Adapt the nothing therein to the purpose in hand, and you will have the use of the cart. Knead clay in order to make a vessel. Adapt the nothing therein to the purpose in hand, and you will have the use of the vessel. Cut out doors and windows in order to make a room. Adapt the nothing therein to the purpose in hand, and you will have the use of the room. Thus what we gain is Something, yet it is by virtue of Nothing that this can be put to use.

An artist who is self-taught is taught by a very ignorant person indeed: Constable

This is Lewis Carroll:

"I see nobody on the road," said Alice.

"I only wish *I* had such eyes," the King remarked in a fretful tone. "To be able to see Nobody! And at that distance too! Why, it's as much as *I* can do to see real people, by this light!"

Is a person who bathes particularly often particularly clean or particularly dirty?

This is "The Fence" by Christian Morgenstern, translated by R. F. C. Hull:

There was a fence with spaces you
Could look through if you wanted to.

An architect who saw this thing
Stood there one summer evening

Took out the spaces with great care
And built a castle in the air.

The fence was utterly dumbfounded—
Each post stood there with nothing round it.

A sight most terrible to see—
They charged it with indecency.

The architect then ran away
To Afric- or Americ-ay.

Impossibility can result from paradox. Here impossibility causes paradox:

Hintikka's paradox

Although it seems clear that what is obligatory must be possible and what is impossible therefore not obligatory, can we say further that what is impossible is not even permissible? Most people's moral intuitions have nothing to say about this, but the following argument, in essence that of Jaako Hintikka, suggests that what is not possible is positively forbidden: It seems clear that

1) to do something which cannot be done without something wrong being done would itself be wrong. But

2) what cannot be done at all cannot be done either with or without something wrong being done—if X is impossible and Y is wrong, I can neither do both X and Y nor do X-but-not-Y.

But by 1), if Y is wrong and doing X-but-not-Y is impossible, it is wrong to do X. Hence,

3) if it is impossible to do X, it is wrong to do it.

In painting you must give the idea of the true by means of the false: Degas

Hempel's paradox of the crows is more concerned with probability than possibility, although he is asking if it is possible to study ornithology indoors. This is the eloquent formulation of Martin Gardner:

"Carl G. Hempel, a leading figure in the 'logical positivist' school and now a professor of philosophy at Princeton University, discovered an astonishing probability paradox. Ever since he first explained it in 1937 in the Swedish periodical 'Theoria,' 'Hempel's Paradox' has been a subject of much learned argument among philosophers of science, for it reaches to the very heart of scientific method.

"Let us assume, Hempel began, that a scientist wishes to investigate the hypothesis 'All crows are black.' His research consists of examining as many crows as possible. The more black crows he finds, the more probable the hypothesis becomes. Each black crow can therefore be regarded as a 'confirming instance' of the hypothesis. Most scientists feel that they have a perfectly clear notion of what a 'confirming instance' is. Hempel's paradox quickly dispels this illusion, for we can easily prove, with ironclad logic, that a purple cow also is a confirming instance of the hypothesis that all crows are black! This is how it is done.

"The statement 'All crows are black' can be transformed, by a process logicians call 'immediate inference,' to the logically equivalent statement, 'All not-black objects are not-crows.' The second statement is identical in meaning with the original; it is simply a different verbal formulation.

70

Obviously, the discovery of any object that confirms the second statement must also confirm the first one.

"Suppose then that the scientist searches about for not-black objects in order to confirm the hypothesis that all such objects are not-crows. He comes upon a purple object. Closer inspection reveals that it is not a crow but a cow. The purple cow is clearly a confirming instance of 'All not-black objects are not-crows.' It therefore must add to the probable truth of the logically equivalent hypothesis, 'All crows are black.' Of course, the same argument applies to a white elephant or a red herring or the scientist's green necktie. As one philosopher recently expressed it, on rainy days an ornithologist investigating the colour of crows could continue his research without getting his feet wet. He has only to glance around his room and note instances of not-black objects that are not-crows!

"As in previous examples of paradoxes, the difficulty seems to lie not in faulty reasoning but in what Hempel calls a 'misguided intuition.' It all begins to make more sense when we consider a simpler example. A company employs a large number of typists, some of whom we know to have red hair. We wish to test the hypothesis that all these red-headed girls are married. An obvious way to do this is to go to each red-headed typist and ask her if she has a husband. But there is another way, and one that might be even more efficient. We obtain from the personnel department a list of all unmarried typists. We then visit the girls

71

on the list to check the colour of their hair. If none have red hair then we have completely confirmed our hypothesis. No one would dispute the fact that each not-married typist who had not-red hair would be a confirming instance of the theory that the firm's red-headed typists are all married.

"There is little difficulty in accepting this investigative procedure because the sets with which we are dealing have a small number of members. But if we are trying to determine whether all crows are black, we have an enormous disproportion between the number of crows on the earth and the number of not-black things. Everyone agrees that checking on non-black things is a highly inefficient way to go about the research. The question at issue is a subtler one—whether it is meaningful to say that a purple cow is in some sense a confirming instance. Does it add, at least in dealing with finite sets (infinite sets lead us into murkier waters), an inconceivably small amount to the probability of our original hypothesis? Some logicians think so. Others are not so sure. They point out, for example, that a purple cow can also be shown, by exacting the same reasoning, to be a confirming instance of 'All crows are white.' How can an object's discovery add to the probable truth of two contradictory hypotheses?

"One may be tempted to dismiss Hempel's paradox with a smile and a shrug. It should be remembered, however, that many logical paradoxes which were long regarded as trivial curiosities proved to be enormously important in the development of modern logic. In similar fashion, analyses of Hempel's paradox have already provided valuable insights into the obscure nature of inductive logic, the tool by which all scientific knowledge is obtained."[26]

Here is a discussion of a paradoxical situation that can be met in life, by John Canfield and Patrick McNally.

Paradoxes of self-deception
"When B lies to himself he comes to believe what he knows to be false; to accept this as a description of a fact is to admit a violation of the law of contradiction. An example of a case of self-deception which generates the paradox is this: A woman knows her son is bad, but fools herself into believing he is good. She then believes he is good, but at the same time, in some way or other, knows and believes that he is bad. We thus say, 'She believes her son is wholly good and she believes he is wholly bad.'

"Consider a person who has fooled himself into believing he is a great artist. We say he behaves as if he were a great artist and that in fact he actually believes he is. On the other hand, we say that deep inside or 'in some corner of his mind' he really does not believe he is a great artist. Since he really does not believe it, he does not believe it. Thus from a description of an actual state of affairs we derive:

"1a he believes he is a great artist and he does not believe he is a great artist.

"There are two ways of interpreting 1a, one of which yields a formal contradiction, the other not.

73

"Idiomatically, 'does not believe' is equivalent to 'disbelieves.'

"Thus 1a can be rewritten:

"1b he believes that he is a great artist and he disbelieves that he is a great artist.

"On the other hand if 1a is interpreted as self-contradictory it must be rendered as:

"2 he believes he is a great artist and it is false that he believes he is a great artist, where the second conjunct is simply the negation of the first and means that he has no belief that he is a great artist.

"It is clear, however, that 2 does not fit the case described. The terms 'deep inside' and 'in some corner of his mind' indicate that in some way the person actually disbelieves in his ability (or believes in his inability, from which the disbelief in his ability follows). And as the case is described, it is false that he has no belief in his ability.

"Not 2 but 1b then is a correct description of the artist's state of belief. 1b is obviously not self-contradictory. If there is a paradox involved in this case, then, it is that our description of an actual state of affairs appears logically odd, or appears to be an informal contradiction."[27]

Definition, that favorite topic of the schoolboy debating society, has provided paradox with fertile ground. Besides formulating the liar paradox, Eubulides devised the "sorites," which is also known as the Sophism of the Slippery Slope, and the bald man. Here we give it in J. Moline's formulation, an imagined conversation—one-sided—between Eubulides and Aristotle:

"You, Aristotle, say that virtue is essentially a mean. And you claim that this applies to all of the various virtues as well. Very well. Consider a case in which I am called upon to give a generous gift. Let the man of practical wisdom consider the case and my means, and say what would count as a generous gift. It does not matter what he says or why, for whatever amount he seizes upon as the generous amount for me to give, will lead to a paradox. For suppose the man of practical wisdom in my circumstances would give n drachmas. Giving just as much as the man of practical wisdom would give and would declare to be the mean is you would say, generous. But it is not. For suppose I give just one obol less. Is my gift not generous? Surely you must concede that giving just one obol less than the generous amount is generous, for an obol is a trifle. Yet if we apply the principle you concede a sufficient number of times, it follows that it is generous to give nothing. But this, clearly, is not generosity, but the extreme of meanness. And suppose that I give one obol more than the mean as specified by the man of practical wisdom. I am giving one obol more than the generous amount, but surely my gift is still generous, for again, an obol is a trifle. But if we apply a sufficient number of times the principle that giving one obol more than what is generous is generous, it follows that it is generous to give not n obols, but one's entire fortune. And this is not generosity, but the extreme of prodigality. You define virtue as a mean. But it follows that virtue is both of the ex-

75

tremes. You see, Aristotle, what trouble there is in trying to define sensibles—it always leads to paradox."[28]

A geographical paradox of definition:

The dictionaries define an island as "a body of land completely surrounded by water" and a lake as "a body of water completely surrounded by land." But suppose the Northern Hemisphere were all land, and the Southern Hemisphere all water. Would you call the Northern Hemisphere an island, or would you call the Southern Hemisphere a lake?

This is a paradox of definition:

"Given a written language, how large in terms of the total number of words must a book printed in that language be in order to contain complete information necessary to manufacture the book?"

(N. Rashevsky)[29]

Analysis, like definition, gives rise to paradox on close inspection:

"Let us call what is to be analysed the analysandum, and let us call that which does the analysing the analysands. The analysis then states an appropriate relation of equivalence between the analysandum and the analysands. And the paradox of analysis is to the effect that, if the verbal expression representing the analysandum has the same meaning as the verbal expression representing the analysands,

76

the analysis states a bare identity and is trivial; but if the two verbal expressions do not have the same meaning, the analysis is incorrect."

(C. H. Langford)[30]

Analysis at a sub-atomic level has given rise to the paradoxical Principle of Uncertainty:

Heisenberg's Principle of Uncertainty, which states that events at the atomic level cannot be observed with certainty, can be compared to this: in the world of everyday experience we can observe any phenomenon and measure its properties without influencing the phenomenon in question to any significant extent. To be sure, if we try to measure the temperature of a demitasse with a bathtub thermometer, the instrument will absorb so much heat from the coffee that it will change the coffee's temperature substantially. But with a small chemical thermometer we may get a sufficiently accurate reading. We can measure the temperature of an object as small as a living cell with miniature thermocouple, which has almost negligible heat capacity. But in the atomic world we can never overlook the disturbance caused by the introduction of the measuring apparatus.

The paradox of analysis has been put more forcibly by Charles Fort:

"Darwinism: the fittest survive. What is meant by the fittest? Not the strongest; not the cleverest—weakness and stupidity everywhere survive. There is no way of determin-

77

ing fitness except in that a thing does survive. 'Fitness,' then, is only another name for 'survival.' Darwinism: that survivors survive."[31]

Defining a map by its scale can also give rise to paradox, approaching infinity:

"Edward Kasner had a way of teaching large numbers to children. He would ask them to guess the length of the eastern coast line of the United States. After a 'sensible' guess had been made—say 2,000 miles—he would proceed step by step to point out that this figure increased enormously if you measured the perimeter of each bay and inlet, then that of every projection and curve of each of these, then the distance separating every small particle of coast-line matter, each molecule, atom, etc. Obviously the coast line is as long as you want to make it."[32]

The map gives rise to two important paradoxes, the paradox of the complete map, and the paradox of the inclusive map.

First, the paradox of the complete map in two formulations. This first quotation is given by J. L. Borges, and may be a hoax attribution; we suspect that it is a version by Borges himself of the Carroll given below.

"In that empire, the art of cartography achieved such perfection that the map of one single province occupied the whole of a city, and the map of the empire, the whole of a province. In time, those disproportionate maps failed to satisfy and the schools of cartography sketched a map of the empire which was of the size of the empire and coincided at every point with it. Less addicted to the study of cartography, the following generations comprehended that this dilated map was useless and, not without impiety, delivered it to the inclemencies of the sun and of the winters. In the western deserts there remain piecemeal ruins of the map, inhabited by animals and beggars. In the entire rest of the country there is no vestige left of the geographical disciplines."

(Suarez Miranda, 1658)[33]

This is a passage from Lewis Carroll's *Sylvie and Bruno Concluded*, 1893, which makes a similar point about this map paradox:

"That's another thing we've learned from *your* Nation," said Mein Herr, "map-making. But we've carried it much further than *you*. What do you consider the *largest* map that would be really useful?"

"About six inches to the mile."

"Only *six inches!*" exclaimed Mein Herr. "We very soon got to six *yards* to the mile. Then we tried a *hundred* yards to the mile. And then came the grandest idea of all! We actually made a map of the country, on the scale of *a mile to the mile!*"

"Have you used it much?" I enquired.

"It has never been spread out, yet," said Mein Herr: "the farmers objected: they said it would cover the whole country, and shut out the sunlight! So we now use the country itself, as its own map, and I assure you it does nearly as well."

The paradox of the inclusive map was posed by Josiah Royce, in *The World and the Individual*, 1899:

"Let us imagine that a portion of the soil of England has been levelled off perfectly and that on it a cartographer traces a map of England. The job is perfect; there is no detail of the soil of England, no matter how minute, that is not registered on the map; everything has there its correspondence. This map, in such a case, should contain a map of the map, which should contain a map of the map of the map, and so on to infinity."

Alfred Jarry's definition of his science of 'pataphysics:

"'pataphysics will examine the laws governing exceptions, and will explain the universe supplementary to this one; or, less ambitiously, will describe a universe which can be—and perhaps should be—envisaged in the place of the traditional one, since the laws that are supposed to have been discovered in the traditional universe are also correlations of exceptions, albeit more frequent ones, but in any case accidental data which, reduced to the status of unexceptional exceptions, possess no longer even the virtue of originality."[34]

Of philosophers who have embraced paradox, that is,

who have proposed a paradoxical point of view, there have been six. There is a kind of historical symmetry. As we have seen, in ancient Greece there were Heraclitus and Zeno. In medieval times there were Nicholas of Cusa, the Bishop of Brixen, and Giordano Bruno, who died at the stake for his beliefs. In modern times, there are the French philosopher Stéphane Lupasco and the British George Melhuish.

Here are brief examples of the work of Cusa and Melhuish.

Nicholas of Cusa writes, in his book *Of Learned Ignorance:*

"As I am about to deal with ignorance as the greatest learning, I consider it necessary to determine the precise meaning of the maximum or greatest. We speak of a thing being the greatest or maximum when nothing greater than it can exist. But to one being alone [God. Ed.] does plenitude belong, with the result that unity, which is also being, and the maximum are identical; for if such a unity is itself in every way and entirely without restriction then it is clear that there is nothing to be placed in opposition to it, since it is the absolute maximum. Consequently, the absolute maximum is one and it is all; all things are in it because it is the maximum. Moreover, it is in all things for this reason that the minimum at once coincides with it, since there is nothing that can be placed in opposition to it. Because it is absolute, it is in actuality all possible being, limiting all things and receiving no limitation from any.

"In the second place, just as we have the absolute maximum, which is the absolute entity by which all things are what they are, so we have from it the universal unity of being which is called the maximum effect of the absolute. In consequence, its existence as the universe is finite, and its unity, which could not be absolute, is the relative unity of a plurality. Though this maximum embraces all things in its universal unity, so that all that comes from the absolute is in it and it in all, yet it could not subsist outside the plurality in which it is contained, for this restriction is inseparably bound up with its existence.

"From the self-evident fact that there is gradation from infinite to finite, it is clear that the simple maximum is not to be found where we meet degrees of more and less; for such degrees are finite, whereas the simple maximum is necessarily infinite. It is manifest, therefore, that when anything other than the simple maximum itself is given, it will always be possible to find something greater. Equality, we find, is a matter of degree: with things that are alike one is more equal to this than to that, insofar as they belong, or do not belong, to the same genus or species, or insofar as they are, or are not, related in time, place, or influence. For that reason it is evident that two or more things cannot be so alike and equal that an infinite number of similar objects cannot still be found. No matter, then, how equal the measure and the thing measured are, they will remain for ever different.

82

"A finite intellect, therefore, cannot by means of comparison reach the absolute truth of things. Being by nature indivisible, truth excludes 'more' or 'less,' so that nothing but truth itself can be the exact measure of truth: for instance, that which is not a circle cannot be the measure of a circle, for the nature of a circle is one and indivisible. In consequence, our intellect, which is not the truth, never grasps the truth with such precision that it could not be comprehended with infinitely greater precision. The relationship of our intellect to the truth is like that of a polygon to a circle; the resemblance to the circle grows with the multiplication of the angles of the polygon; but apart from its being reduced to identity with the circle, no multiplication, even if it were infinite, of its angles will make the polygon equal to the circle.

"It is clear, therefore, that all we know of truth is that the absolute truth, such as it is, is beyond our reach. The truth, which can be neither more nor less than it is, is the most absolute necessity, while, in contrast with it, our intellect is possibility. Therefore, the quiddity of things, which is ontological truth, is unattainable in its entirety; and though it has been the objective of all philosophers, by none has it been found as it really is. The more profoundly we learn this lesson of ignorance, the closer we draw to truth itself."[35]

The contemporary British philosopher George Melhuish has written the following piece exemplifying his paradoxical philosophy, especially for this book:

In order to define the innate flux of things, it is necessary to state a fundamental paradox and to say that what is the same as itself is in self-modification, whereby it is not the same as itself, for any less paradoxical operation will commit us to the acceptance of a merely static identity and this will imply that different things will not need to be in a state of change in order not to be the same. If we say dogmatically that something involved in change really amounts to different things, then these things will have independent and simple existence, and will not be actually involved in change. Certainly, by ordinary logical standards to say that the thing which is the same as itself is actually in self-modification whereby it is not the same as itself will appear unacceptably contradictory: but this does not imply an impossibility.

To establish an adequate logic of change, we need to call upon a logic both ordered and not ordered by the basic principles of identity and non-contradiction. For us, at least, the most central and most crucial state, wherein change occurs, is to be found in the cradle of experience. It is necessary to see that logic is developed adequately only by a contradictory complementarity implying paradoxical coalescence. The total abrogation of identity would deprive us of our whole system of identification; yet to hold dogmatically to the principle of identity will be to maintain a merely static order where flux remains unexpressed and undefined. Only by the affirmation of the orthodox conceptual scheme and its abrogation, by a really antithetical conceptual scheme, will change be defined.

In order to define the innate flux of things, it is necessary to state a fundamental paradox and to say that what is the same as itself is in self-modification, whereby it is not the same as itself, for any less paradoxical operation will commit us to the acceptance of a merely static identity and this will imply that different things will not need to be in a state of change in order not to be the same. If we say dogmatically that something involved in change really amounts to different things, then these things will have independent and simple existence, and will not be actually involved in change. Certainly, by ordinary logical standards to say that the thing which is the same as itself is actually in self-modification whereby it is not the same as itself will appear unacceptably contradictory: but this does not imply an impossibility.

To establish an adequate logic of change, we need to call upon a logic both ordered and not ordered by the basic principles of identity and non-contradiction. For us, at least, the most central and most crucial state, wherein change occurs, is to be found in the cradle of experience. It is necessary to see that logic is developed adequately only by a contradictory complementarity implying paradoxical coalescence. The total abrogation of identity would deprive us of our whole system of identification; yet to hold dogmatically to the principle of identity will be to maintain a merely static order where flux remains unexpressed and undefined. Only by the affirmation of the orthodox conceptual scheme and its abrogation, by a really antithetical conceptual scheme, will change be defined.

84

Obviously, abrogation of the logical principles of identity and contradiction must appear very strange. In ordinary terminology, two-oneness will imply an extension in complexity beyond the mere simplicity of one, and as such, one signifies something *more simple* than two-one. However, when we speak to establish the true metaphysical significance of change, the fact of two-one is as irreducible as one.

The contradiction that is established causes us to say that not only the thing which is the same as itself is changing, but that the significance that is the same as itself is changing too. Hence not only as an empirical fact is the thing which is the same as itself changing, but significance is changing also. Obviously we need a state of identity and non-contradiction in order that things may have selectivity and particularity, but whereas it has been usual to accept that tautological principles of logic represent sufficient necessitation on which to base the conceptual scheme, we must now see that an adequate definition of the reality of occurrence erects *actual contradiction* and actual *non-identity*. The state of experience commits us to a significance wherein contradiction and non-identity are actualities, not mere negations. Hence the necessity of a paradoxical state that is energetic.

In virtue of its pure change, the primordial flux of experience completely eludes orthodox logical interpretation. In fact, as the subject matter of the experiential matrix is what it is, it is already something else. At the center of the matrix of perception we are confronted with an actual contradiction, but an actual paradox capable of formalization into a logic of contradiction is something radically different from mere self-contradiction, implying error or meaninglessness. Modern philosophers have been neglectful of actual contradiction, therefore it appears entirely strange to established modes of thought.

In fact we must break completely with the long-standing logical tradition based upon the unambiguous nature of identity and its legislation by the law of non-contradiction. However, this does not imply that the traditional conceptual scheme is rendered effete, since in its rightful place orthodox logic remains a central necessity. But it is incumbent upon us to see that with regard to the ultimate nature of things the central tautologies of accepted logic represent only half of the logical truth; the other half being represented by a non-static anti-identity logical order in the guise of an energetic state, which implies basic disruption of the central tautologies of accepted logic.

Orthodox logic has been content to accept only a tautological framework wherein things are brought down to logically unparadoxical proportions. However, it is necessary for us to accept the logical form for the embracement of a non-tautological and paradoxically energetic reality. The condition which we need to consider is that in which the states of presence and absence exist at the level of an energetic binary, so constituting the vehicle for the subject matter of all experiential occurrence. The term "subject of experience" is here bifurcated into "the subject as merely itself" *and* "the subject as not merely itself." In order to follow this new logical ambiguity it is necessary to see that the marriage between the subject matter of experience and its vehicle cannot be defined by a non-paradoxical single-order definition. If we wish to expose logically the dynamic state of experiential occurrence it is necessary to say that any definition of subject matter necessitates a vehicle whereby the states of presence and absence are energetically opposed.

Because what we begin with cannot be less than a primordial flux, it must be our aim to rationalize innate change. The pulsation of the experiential moment always involves some subject matter, but since as something governed by identity each subject matter is static, pulsation itself can never be reliant for its initial force upon any one particular kind of subject matter; and yet within the experiential moments all subject matter occurs energetically. In fact the subject and the vehicle upon which it attempts to rest cannot be only in a simple and non-paradoxical one-to-one correspondence, because if this was the case we should be stranded with something less than pure dynamics. There is definite coalescence between subject and vehicle, but their coming together represents a meeting in actual disruption.

The duration of the presence of any subject in flux must fall necessarily short of what "the subject as merely itself" would need to imply. By the standard of orthodox logic,

"the subject as merely itself" must be instantaneous with itself and possess a presence exactly equal to itself; it must be
exactly where it is, since conventionally speaking there is
nothing else it can be. But we see that such identities pre-
clude the logical definition of change. When we define the
elements of experience at a truly energetic level, subject
matter must be one mutually exclusive category and its vehicle the other. For the *energetic* presence and absence of
subject matter we are referring to that part of experience
"which is not a subject." In fact, in order to define primordial flux, we need to maintain the experiential subject
as never less than both present *and* absent; thus we are af-
firming the energetic coalescence of presence *and* absence.

The paradoxical coalescence of presence and absence involves all subject matter irrespective of type: thus rational
affirmations and denials as well as phenomenological objects and sensa qualify as subject matter used by the energetic vehicle. By the standards of the paradoxically energetic state to say that something is present is to imply always
presence and absence; and through being available to be
both present *and* absent all subject matter occurs at the
level of a paradoxically energetic indeterminacy.

In speaking of the active occurrence of experience, we
imply a situation that is both compact and expansive. We
can speak of a particular experience, but if our awareness
was limited to only one simple thing there would in fact be
no experience at all. It is a condition of experience that
what occurs is always more than any one thing; that is to

say, more than any one thing given by the standard principle of identity. If "the subject as merely itself" equals "the subject as not merely itself" it is necessary to see that this is because "the subject as merely itself" has been induced to fall short of actual presence to the degree whereby there is also an actual absence and thereby a logically paradoxical two-oneness.

In fact the state of flux necessary to the arc of actualization whereby consciousness or experience is exposed erects an authentic confusion through which the subject as a mere simple is equally not a mere simple. Only in the tautological logic will it be correct to equate dogmatically a whole within a whole, or a one with a one and thereby any thing merely with the fact of itself. In non-tautological logic a whole or a one equates with its antithesis through being "more than a whole," "more than a one." In the experiential state no particular thing defined is only itself, and in not being limited to itself the moment of actualization is rendered ambiguous and never still.[36]

To conclude, here are some remarks of Philip Wheelright:

"Now ordinary paradox, or paradox of surface, is merely a trick of speech whereby a point can be made more wittily and effectively. 'Christ was no Christian,' 'Freud was no Freudian,' 'Nothing is more fatiguing than leisure,' or Chesterton's 'Nothing is so miraculous as the commonplace'— such paradoxes as these may grace an evening's conversation and give the perpetrator a reputation for cleverness,

89

but actually they depend for their effect upon a more or less deliberate confusion between two connotations of a word— e.g., between Christianity as it is practiced and Christianity defined as adhering to the principles of its founder, or between genuine leisure and the sheer inoccupancy in which one burdens oneself with trifles, or between the dramatic sort of miracle that involves a breaking away from the commonplace and the ultimate metaphysical miracle that existence and order should be instead of nonexistence and chaos.[37]

"By contrast, a radical and serious paradox does not hang upon a removable confusion, but is demanded by the complexity and inherent ambiguity of what is being expressed."[38]

If you work on your mind with your mind, how can you avoid an immense confusion: Seng-Ts'an

FOOTNOTES

1. Page 126 of *The Hole, and Other Plays and Sketches* by N. F. Simpson, London, 1964.

2. From *Catch-22* by Joseph Heller, New York, 1961.

3. Thomas Storer, *Analysis,* June 1962, pages 151–52.

4. A. P. Ushenko, "A Note on the Liar Paradox," *Mind,* October 1955.

5. P. E. B. Jourdain, "Tales with Philosophical Morals," *The Open Court,* vol. 27 (1913), pages 310–15, Chicago.

6. In a letter to *The Listener,* London, July 23, 1970. There was an interesting correspondence in this weekly journal between June 4 and August 20, 1970, about this paradox.

7. Martin Gardner, "Logical Paradoxes," *Antioch Review,* Summer 1963.

8. In a letter to *The Listener,* London, July 9, 1970.

9. Bertrand Russell, *My Philosophical Development,* London, 1959.

10. Bertrand Russell, *The Autobiography of Bertrand Russell,* vol. 1, London, 1967.

11. Max Black has proposed this variant: **The least integer not named in this book.**

12. J. A. Benardete, *Infinity,* © Oxford University Press. Oxford, 1964, page 1.

If I am I because you are you, and if you are you because I am I,
then I am not I, and you are not you: Hasidic rabbi

13. Alan R. White, *Mind,* January 1963.

14. This can be compared with Eubulides' sorites, or heap, paradox. It is given in the form of a paradox about generosity on page 75. Eubulides originally proposed that there can be no such thing as a heap of sand since one grain does not make a heap and adding one grain is never enough to convert a non-heap into a heap.

15. J. A. Benardete, *Infinity,* Oxford, 1964, page 9.

16. Ibid., page 21.

17. Ibid., page 236.

18. Ibid., page 259.

19. Ibid., page 252 and following.

20. P. E. B. Jourdain, *The Philosophy of Mr. B*rtr*nd R*ss*ll,* London, 1918, page 66 and following.

21. Max Black, *Problems of Analysis,* London, 1954, page 102.

22. Ibid., page 103.

23. Ibid., page 104.

24. It now seems that this paradox may have its origin in a Swedish broadcast announcement, in 1943 or 1944, that a civil-defense exercise would be held the following week, and to test the efficiency of civil-defense units, no one would be able to predict, even on the morning of the day of the exercise, when it would take place. Lennart Ekbom realized that this involved a logical paradox.

25. E. V. Milner, *Mind,* 1967.

26. Martin Gardner, *Mathematical Puzzles and Diversions,* London, 1961, page 54 and following.

27. John Canfield and Patrick McNally, "Paradoxes of Self-Deception," *Analysis*, 1961.

28. J. Moline, "Aristotle, Eubulides and the Sorites," *Mind*, July 1969.

29. N. Rashevsky, "Life, Information Theory and Topology," *Bulletin of Mathematics and Metaphysics*, 17, 1955.

30. C. H. Langford, "The Notion of Analysis in Moore's Philosophy," *The Philosophy of G. E. Moore*, ed. P. A. Schlipp, page 323.

31. Charles Fort, *The Books of Charles Fort*, New York, 1941, page 23.

32. Quoted by Clifton Fadiman in the introduction to *The Mathematical Magpie*, New York, 1962.

33. Quoted by J. L. Borges and A. B. Casares in *Extraordinary Tales*, London, 1973.

34. Roger Shattuck and Simon Watson Taylor (eds.), *Selected Works of Alfred Jarry*, London, 1965, page 196.

35. Nicholas of Cusa, *Of Learned Ignorance*, London, 1954. This work was completed in 1440.

36. George Melhuish's latest book is *The Paradoxical Nature of Reality*, Bristol, 1973.

37. When a paradox is compressed into two contradictory words as in "loud silence," "lonely crowd," or "living death," it is called an *oxymoron*.

38. Philip Wheelwright, *Heraclitus*, Princeton, 1959, page 98.

BIBLIOGRAPHY

The Vicious Circle in Logic

RUSSELL, B., and WHITEHEAD, A. N.	*Principia Mathematica.* Cambridge, 1910.
RUSTOW, A.	*Der Lügner: Theorie, Geschichte und Auflösung.* Leipzig, 1910.
JOURDAIN, P. E. B.	*The Philosophy of Mr. B*rtr*nd R*ss*ll.* London, 1918.
GRELLING, K.	"The Logical Paradoxes." *Mind,* 1936.
USHENKO, A. P.	*The Problems of Logic.* Princeton, 1941.
KOYRÉ, A.	*Épiménide le Menteur.* Paris, 1947.
LANGFORD, C. H.	"On a Certain Modal Proposition." *Mind,* 1947.
LANGFORD, C. H.	"On Paradoxes of the Type of the Epimenides." *Mind,* 1947.
GREGORY, J. C.	"Heterological and Homological." *Mind,* 1952.
USHENKO, A. P.	"A Note on the Liar Paradox." *Mind,* 1955.
KEMPNER, A. J.	*Paradoxes and Common Sense.* New York, 1959.
QUINE, W. V. O.	"Paradox." *Scientific American,* 1962.
TOMS, E.	*Being, Negation, and Logic.* Oxford, 1962.
POPPER, K.	*Conjectures and Refutations.* London, 1963.
GRIDGEMAN, N. T.	"The Pit of Paradox." *New Scientist,* 1963.

TEENSMA, E.	*The Paradoxes.* Assen, 1969.
TARSKI, A.	"Truth and Proof, the Antinomy of the Liar . . ." *Scientific American,* 1969.
(Various)	*The Listener,* May 14 to August 20, 1970.
MARTIN, R. L.	*The Paradox of the Liar.* Yale, 1970.
UL-HAQUE, I.	*A Critical Study of Logical Paradoxes.* Peshawar, 1970.
BARTLEY, W. W.	"Lewis Carroll's Lost Book on Logic." *Scientific American,* 1972.
MACKIE, J. L.	*Truth, Probability, and Paradox.* Oxford, 1973.

The Paradoxes of Infinity

CARROLL, L. (DODGSON, C. L.)	"What the Tortoise Said to Achilles." *Mind,* 1895.
RUSSELL, B.	*Principles of Mathematics.* London, 1903.
ARISTOTLE.	*Physics.* London, 1929.
LEE, H. N. P.	*Zeno of Elea.* Cambridge, 1936.
BOLZANO, B.	*The Paradoxes of the Infinite.* London, 1951.
RYLE, G.	*Dilemmas.* Cambridge, 1954.
KIRK, G. S., and RAVEN, J. E.	*The Presocratic Philosophers.* Cambridge, 1957.
OWEN, G. E. L.	"Zeno and the Mathematicians." *Proceedings of the Aristotelian Society,* 1957–58.
PASSMORE, J.	*Philosophical Reasoning.* London, 1961.
GAMOW, G.	*One, Two, Three . . . Infinity.* New York, 1947.

GARDNER, M. "Some Paradoxes and Puzzles Involving Infinite Series and the Concept of Limit." *Scientific American,* 1964.

GARDNER, M. "The Infinite Regress . . ." *Scientific American,* 1965.

WOODS, J. "Was Achilles' 'Achilles' Heel' Achilles' Heel?" *Analysis,* 1965.

GARDNER, M. "The Hierarchy of Infinities and the Problems It Spawns." *Scientific American,* 1966.

GRUNBAUM, A. *Modern Science and Zeno's Paradoxes.* Middletown, 1967.

HARRISON, A. "Zeno's Paper Chase." *Mind,* 1967.

NORTHROP, E. *Riddles in Mathematics.* London, 1967.

KASTNER, E., and NEWMAN, J. *Mathematics and the Imagination.* London, 1968.

SALMON, W. *Zeno's Paradoxes.* New York, 1970.

The Surprise Inspection Paradox

O'CONNOR, D. J. "Pragmatic Paradoxes." *Mind,* July 1948.

COHEN, L. J. "Mr. O'Connor's Pragmatic Paradoxes." *Mind,* January 1950.

ALEXANDER, P. J. "Pragmatic Paradoxes." *Mind,* October, 1950.

SCRIVEN, M. "Paradoxical Announcements." *Mind,* July 1951.

O'CONNOR, D. J. "Pragmatic Paradoxes, and Fugitive Propositions." *Mind,* October 1951.

WEISS, P. "The Prediction Paradox." *Mind,* April 1952.

QUINE, W. V. O. — "On a So-Called Paradox." *Mind,* January 1953.

SHAW, R. — "The Paradox of the Unexpected Examination." *Mind,* July 1958.

LYON, A. — "The Prediction Paradox." *Mind,* October 1959.

KAPLAN, D., and MONTAGUE, R. — "A Paradox Regained." *Notre Dame Journal of Formal Logic,* July 1960.

O'BEIRNE, T. H. — "Can the Unexpected Never Happen?" *New Scientist,* May 1961.

NERLICH, G. C. — "Unexpected Examinations and Unprovable Statements." *Mind,* October 1961.

GARDNER, M. — "A New Prediction Paradox." *British Journal for the Philosophy of Science,* 1962.

POPPER, K. R. — "A Comment on the New Prediction Paradox." *British Journal for the Philosophy of Science,* 1962.

GARDNER, M. — "A New Paradox, and Variations on It, About a Man Condemned to Be Hanged." *Scientific American,* March 1963.

MEDLIN, B. — "The Unexpected Examination." *American Philosophical Quarterly,* January 1964.

SHARPE, R. A. — "The Unexpected Examination." *Mind,* April 1965.

CHAPMAN, J. M., and BUTLER, R. J. — "On Quine's So-Called Paradox." *Mind,* July 1965.

KIEFER, J., and ELLISON, J. — "The Prediction Paradox Again." *Mind,* July 1965.

SCHOENBERG, J. — "A Note on the Logical Fallacy in the Paradox of the Unexpected Examination." *Mind,* January 1966.

"Extremes meet," as the whiting said with its tail in its mouth: Thomas Hood

WRIGHT, J. A.   "The Surprise Exam: Prediction on Last Day Uncertain." *Mind*, January 1967.

Paradox in Philosophy

LUPASCO, S.   *Logique et Contradiction.* Paris, 1947.
LUPASCO, S.   *Le Principe d'Antagonisme et la Logique de l'Énergie.* Paris, 1951.
CUSA, N.   *Of Learned Ignorance.* London, 1954.
MELHUISH, G.   *The Paradoxical Universe.* Bristol, 1959.
WHEELWRIGHT, P.   *Heraclitus.* Princeton, 1959.
SLAATTE, H. A.   *The Pertinence of the Paradox.* New York, 1968.
MELHUISH, G.   *The Paradoxical Nature of Reality.* Bristol, 1973.
LUPASCO, S.   *L'Énergie et la Matière Psychique.* Paris, 1974.

Paradox in General

KENNER, H.   *Paradox in Chesterton.* London, 1948.
FADIMAN, C.   *Fantasia Mathematica.* New York, 1958.
KEMPNER, A. J.   *Paradoxes and Common Sense.* New York, 1959.
BOMBAUGH, C. C.   *Oddities and Curiosities of Words and Literature.* New York, 1961.
FADIMAN, C.   *The Mathematical Magpie.* New York, 1962.
GARDNER, M.   "Logical Paradoxes." *Antioch Review,* 1963.

Great fleas have little fleas upon their backs to bite 'em and little fleas have lesser fleas and so ad infinitum: Augustus De Morgan

ALLEN, R. R.   *Bible Paradoxes.* Michigan, 1963.
COLIE, R. L.   *Paradoxica Epidemica: The Renaissance Tradition of Paradox.* Princeton, 1966.
HAMBLIN, C. L.   *Fallacies.* London, 1970.

ILLUSTRATION CREDITS

1. A page from a booklet entitled *Watching Words Move,* by the graphic designers Brownjohn, Chermayeff, and Geismar.

2. "Cadeau" ("Gift"), by Man Ray, 1921.

3. Fur cup, saucer, and spoon, by Méret Oppenheim, 1936.

4. "La Trahison des Images" ("The Treachery of Images"), oil painting by René Magritte, 1928 or 1929. From the collection of William Copley, New York.

5. "Cloakroom Ticket," drawing by Patrick Hughes, 1962.

6. "Drawing Hands," lithograph by M. C. Escher, 1948. From the Escher Foundation, Haags Gemeentemuseum, The Hague.

7. "La Condition Humaine" ("The Human Condition"), oil painting by René Magritte, 1936. From the collection of Claude Spaak, Paris.

8. A still from the film *Les Violons d'Ingres* (*Ingres' Violins*), directed by Jacques Brunius, 1939.

9. A photograph originally published in *Foundations of Modern Art,* by Ozenfant, in 1928.

10. "Les Jours Gigantesques" ("Gigantic Days"), drawing by René Magritte.

11. Contemporary copy of a drawing by Dürer of the ouroboros.

12. "Endless Snake," painted ceramic sculpture by Patrick Hughes, 1969. Photograph by John Timbers.

13. Object designed and made by Malcolm Fowler of Shirtsleeve Studio, London, 1970.

14. "Short Circuit," object by Patrick Hughes, 1971. Photograph by John Timbers.

15. Photograph of eighty people (including Patrick Hughes in white suit at the front) setting the then world record for an "unsupported circle" on May 22, 1973. Photograph by courtesy of John Timbers. (See *Guinness Book of Records,* London, 1972, page 233.)

16. The Möbius strip, a band with a half twist, first described by the German mathematician Ferdinand Möbius in 1858.

17. The Penrose triangle, published by L. S. Penrose and R. Penrose in their paper "Impossible Objects," *British Journal of Experimental Psychology,* 1956.

18. A Möbius strip with three half twists, flattened to form a triangle.

19. The Penrose staircase, published by L. S. Penrose and R. Penrose in 1956. The model was made by May and Baker Ltd., chemical manufacturers of Dagenham, Essex.

20. Another view of May and Baker's model.

21. "Ascending and Descending," lithograph by M. C. Escher, 1960. From the Escher Foundation, Haags Gemeentemuseum, The Hague.

22. A poster for the Holland Book Fair designed by Total Design, Holland.

23. "Infinity," painting by Patrick Hughes, 1970. From the collection of Lord and Lady Beaumont of Whitley, London.

102

24. "L'Objet" ("The Object"), collage by Marcel Mariën. From the collection of Christian Bussy, Brussels.

25. "Hull," drawing by Patrick Hughes, 1973. From the collection of the Ferens Art Gallery, Hull.

26. A photograph taken by James B. Hyzer (at the age of twelve).

The paradoxes listed below are given in the words of the writers credited:

p. 3 Gardner's "lawyer" paradox: Martin Gardner, *The Antioch Review*, Summer 1963, p. 174.

pp. 3–4 The "crocodile" paradox: ibid., p. 174.

p. 4 The "lawyer/student" paradox: ibid., p. 174.

p. 4 The "poacher" paradox: Edward Kasner and James Newman, *Mathematics and the Imagination*, Harmondsworth, 1968, p. 187.

p. 5 The "Sancho Panza" paradox: Martin Gardner, op. cit., p. 175.

p. 5 The "Groucho Marx" paradox: ibid., p. 175.

pp. 5–6 The "jail" paradox: C. C. Bombaugh *Oddities and Curiosities of Words and Literature,* ed. Martin Gardner, New York, 1961 (first published 1890), p. 253.

p. 10 Jourdain's "card" paradox: Martin Gardner, op. cit., p. 174.

pp. 14–15 Berry's paradox: Bertrand Russell and A. N. Whitehead, *Principia Mathematica*, Cambridge, 1910, p. 61.

p. 16 Mailer's paradox: Martin Gardner, "The Infinite Regress . . ." *Scientific American*, April 1965, p. 130.

pp. 16–17 The "putting the motion" paradox: ibid., p. 128, quoting "from an old issue of *Punch.*"

p. 18 The "third man" paradox: ibid., p. 128.

p. 18 The "first cause" paradox: ibid., p. 128.

p. 19 Zeno's first argument against plurality: Gregory Vlastos, "Zeno," in The Encyclopedia of Philosophy, Vol. 8, New York, 1967, p. 369.

p. 21 Zeno's second argument against plurality: ibid., p. 371.

p. 21 Zeno's third argument against plurality: ibid., p. 371.

p. 22 Zeno's "race course" paradox: J. A. Benardete, *Infinity*, Oxford, 1964, p. 1

p. 26 Zeno's "arrow" paradox: G. E. L. Owen, "Zeno and the Mathematicians," in *Proceedings of the Aristotelian Society*, 1957–58, p. 216.

p. 27 Zeno's "moving blocks" paradox: ibid., p. 208.

pp. 33–34 Cantor's paradoxical arithmetic: George Gamow, *One, Two, Three . . . Infinity*, New York, 1967, pp. 16–24.

pp. 34–35 Hilbert's "Grand Hotel" paradox: ibid., p. 17.

p. 39 The Thomson lamp: Martin Gardner, "The orders of infinity . . . ," *Scientific American*, March 1971, p. 107.

pp. 39–40 Black's paradoxes: quoted in Adolf Grunbaum, *Modern Science and Zeno's Paradoxes,* Middletown, 1967, p. 81 et. seq.

p. 69 Hintikka's paradox: A. N. Prior, "Deontic Logic," in the Encyclopedia of Philosophy, Vol. 4, New York, 1967, p. 511.

p. 77 Heisenberg's Principle of Uncertainty: George Gamow, "The Principle of Uncertainty," *Scientific American* offprint, 1958, p. 3.

Q